THE
EXCEPTIONALS

Kumar Mehta is the author of the number one Amazon bestseller, *The Innovation Biome*, and has been at the forefront of research, innovation and data analytics for 30 years. He researches, writes and speaks about personal excellence and innovation, and his professional experience includes nine years as the CEO of a large data analytics company and a 14-year stint at Microsoft.

Dr Mehta also serves as a senior research fellow at the Center for the Digital Future at the University of Southern California. He is passionate about education and serves as treasurer for the Committee for Children (CFC), a global non-profit dedicated to fostering the safety and well-being of children through social-emotional learning and development.

He holds a PhD in pharmaceutical socioeconomics from The University of Iowa and lives in Seattle.

'Dr Mehta is a brilliant researcher and writer. For years, he has been studying the integrated nature of how talent manifests itself in people and how to reach that possible best. *The Exceptionals* gives us a clear pathway to achieve greatness.

—**Gabe Jaramillo,** coach to 11 world #1 tennis players and 27 world top 10 players

'*The Exceptionals* by Kumar Mehta is a fascinating and comprehensive look at the commonalities in individuals who have reached an elite level in various professions. This book can serve as a roadmap for coaches and leaders as we try and facilitate sustained excellence in those we mentor.'

—**Julianne Benson,** 1996 Olympian and professional track and field coach

'It was an honour to be one of the first to read *The Exceptionals*. I am training an exceptional, so this was an incredibly useful read for me. Kumar Mehta has done an amazing job explaining what it takes to become the best of the best, and I have no doubt that you will surely benefit from reading this book, whether you are working with exceptional talent or not.'

—**Peter Andrew,** coach (and dad) to world champion swimmer Michael Andrew and head coach of The New York Breakers elite swim team.

'Dr Kumar Mehta captures the layers of success that drive a person to become exceptional. In baseball terms, we would say that he has identified and explained the sixth tool. This book is an exceptional read for understanding the traits required to become an accomplished professional athlete—or just as successful in any other field of life.'

—**Jeffrey Cirillo,** 14-year Major League Baseball player, MLB record holder for consecutive errorless games, and MLB scout

'When I read *The Exceptionals*, I thought it was almost a God's gift that I could have content like this available to help me guide my students and children to achieve success. What I took away from the book was how you can become a world changer. I especially loved the idea of 'microexcellence.'

I was so excited and inspired after reading the book that I asked my two sons to read one chapter a day and then process the information and prepare a summary that we could discuss. I think this book is going to play an instrumental role in their development. It provides us with the blueprint on what to focus on.'

—**Sam Frost,** long-time coach of multiple major winners on the PGA, LPGA, European, and Asian Tours, and coach (and dad) of two upcoming junior golfers.

'*The Exceptionals* is a comprehensive guide to the intangibles that help make the 1% of the 1% exactly that. This book will serve as a great inspiration to those just beginning the path towards exceptionalism. Through inspiring anecdotes and a well-mapped guide to achieving one's goals, this book helps spring the motivated individual into action—"because lost time is the only thing you cannot make up."'

—**Jacob Nissly,** principal percussionist, San Francisco Symphony

'Dr Mehta's book deciphers the key insights to being exceptional. It is a must-read for helping you be your best and at the top of your field.'

—**Brad Chase,** author of Strategy First: *How Businesses Win Big*

'*The Exceptionals* will inspire talented individuals to reach for their highest level.'

—**Julie Landsman,** former principal horn with the Metropolitan Opera and master teacher at The Julliard School and USC Thornton School

THE
EXCEPTIONALS

HOW THE BEST BECOME THE BEST
AND HOW YOU CAN TOO

KUMAR MEHTA

RUPA

Published by
Rupa Publications India Pvt. Ltd 2021
7/16, Ansari Road, Daryaganj
New Delhi 110002

Sales centres:
Allahabad Bengaluru Chennai
Hyderabad Jaipur Kathmandu
Kolkata Mumbai

This edition for the Indian subcontinent has been published by
special arrangement with River Grove Books Austin, TX.

The views and opinions expressed in this book are the
author's own and the facts are as reported by him which
have been verified to the extent possible, and the publishers
are not in any way liable for the same.

ISBN: 978-93-90918-16-4

First impression 2021

10 9 8 7 6 5 4 3 2 1

The moral right of the author has been asserted.

For Curren, Priyanka and Reuben—and your generation.

CONTENTS

INTENSE EFFORT

JOINING HE EXCEPTIONALS

PREFACE

THE 1% OF THE 1%

Humans are not equal. There are a few individuals who have achieved an unparalleled mastery in their field, and they are who I call *the exceptionals*. They are the people who have succeeded in being able to draw out the best talents they have within themselves. They are the ones who have raised the bar so high that very few can achieve what they have achieved. In short, they have maximized the physical, mental and social potential available to them.

Being exceptional is rare. We often talk about the top 1 per cent, which translates to about 3.3 million people in the United States. And while being in the top 1 per cent in anything is a fantastic accomplishment that most of us never achieve, being exceptional means being closer to the 1 per cent of the 1 per cent; it is far more selective. This is the *permyriad*—the one in 10,000. The permyriad includes approximately 30,000 especially spectacular individuals in the country who have scaled the peak in every profession.

The reason for a focus on this small and exclusive group of individuals is to be able to get a deep understanding of the foundational elements of excellence that are common across the most elite individuals. If we understand the traits that are common across the exceptionals, we can apply them to our lives. We all start with varying levels of natural abilities and talent, so even if everything else is the same, different outcomes are to be expected. But if we apply the universal principles of sustained excellence to our lives, we will be able to achieve our *possible best* all the time. When we attain our possible best, we too have the potential to become exceptional and reach the top of our profession, whatever it may be.

Achieving your possible best gives you the satisfaction of knowing you gave it your all. There are no regrets, and you live up to the wise words of Dr Martin Luther King Jr.: 'Don't just set out to do a good job. Set out to do such a good job that the living, the dead or the unborn couldn't do it any better.' Only when you live up to this ethos can you hope to become exceptional.

The road to sustained excellence varies for everyone. It is not linear, and there is no direct path that can get you there. It is created and shaped by raw abilities, individual experiences, environments and unique moments. The first thing I wish to communicate through this book is that becoming exceptional is multifaceted. It is a combination of several different dimensions that we will discuss. All of them are necessary to achieve extraordinary results.

THE PATH TO EXCELLENCE

This book is intended to give you a roadmap or a blueprint for you to achieve sustained excellence. The effort to develop this blueprint has been three years in the making. The process started with a series of conversations and interviews with many exceptionals in a variety of fields, including Nobel laureates, world-class athletes and musicians, and people in other professions who reached the very elite levels in their fields. I tried to understand their lives and their stories and how they were able to scale the pyramid when many others could not. As I spoke with more people, themes started to emerge. Exceptional individuals from all walks of life were using the same concepts, and sometimes even the same words, as they described what got them to the top.

Additionally, I studied the growth and development of many people who have reached the top rungs in their fields. Some of these people are household names, while others come from areas that often don't make the headlines but require the same qualities of extreme success. I have studied a vast number of interviews to understand the factors that helped them develop into the most extraordinary individuals the world has seen.

Finally, the field of what it takes to become exceptional has been researched extensively by scholars around the world for decades. I have studied countless research papers and articles on what other researchers have learned, all of which have further shaped my thinking.

The themes shared in this book have come from my

deep immersion into the topic and from synthesizing information from all possible sources. I am confident that the essential elements for developing a blueprint for becoming exceptional are covered in this book.

There are many books available that attempt to explain the traits required to become exceptional. I have learned from them, but invariably these books rest on a single principle, and often that unique principle conflicts with the beliefs offered in other books.

Some books may tell you that extraordinary performance is genetic, whereas others say your genes are mostly irrelevant, and through hard work and dedication, you can attain anything. In my opinion, both points of view are oversimplifications of what becoming exceptional is all about. Some writers may tell you that you need to put the time and effort into a single activity, whereas others say you become excellent by focusing on multiple things. I believe both points of view are valid, but they don't go far enough, because achieving excellence requires so much more.

There is a vast body of work done on this topic by many smart people. I hope to add to that discussion.

I believe there is a specific area where each and every one of you can excel, so the first thing you should do to achieve sustained excellence is find the domain that allows your innate abilities to shine through. Once you are in the right field, you will need to put in an incredible amount of effort to become exceptional. Finally, you will need to adopt the set of enabling factors that have been present on every journey to the top. These three elements (innate abilities, intense effort and enabling factors) make up the formula for sustained excellence.

This book not only discusses these three elements, but it also brings forward ways (rooted in research and science) you can apply these elements to your life. This book is not purely an academic discussion or a thought-provoking piece on the attributes of excellence; it shows you how you can do it. It provides you with your blueprint to achieve whatever you dream of attaining.

The qualities that allow you to reach your possible best in one field translate well to other domains. I have come across many people who were up-and-coming musicians or athletes, and at one point they all shared a dream of becoming the very best in the world at their craft.

For any of several reasons, they did not quite make it to the world stage. But their quest to achieve their possible best led them to have immensely successful, fulfilling and rewarding careers in other professions, with many becoming successful lawyers, physicians or leaders in business. Today, they attribute much of their current success to the lessons learned while on their journey to achieving their possible best at their initial craft. The qualities that are required to make you exceptional cut across disciplines, and they are transferable. This means the things you learn as you develop in one area are relevant to attaining success in another field. The domains may be different, and the specific expertise required to excel may be different. But the process of honing your skills and maximizing the potential of your abilities translates well across disciplines.

WHY STRIVE TO BE THE BEST OF THE BEST?

If the ultimate goal of life is to be happy, should you strive to become exceptional? Will it make you happier? Humans, by nature, are driven. That is why we strive to get better, run faster, jump higher, create more value, save more lives and excel in every way imaginable. Achieving goals and fulfilling our potential is what we all strive for. Most people want to be the best at what they do. Every parent wants their children to achieve their full potential, and every leader wants their team to operate at its peak capability.

In our society, being exceptional is outstandingly rewarded. Take financial rewards, for example. If you are the best of the best, you don't just earn five times the average; you earn 50 times or 100 times the average. Whether right or wrong, our society has developed a system where exceptional performance has disproportionately high rewards.

Being the best often means earning a lot of money, but the question is: *Will it make you happy?* While we live by the common refrain that money can't buy happiness, research in the area has shown that achieving great wealth does in fact tend to make you happier.[1] The caveat is that great wealth can make you happy only if you have earned it yourself (as opposed to inheriting it or coming into a windfall). People with a net worth of greater than

---

[1] Grant E. Donnelly, T. Zhang, E. Haisley, and M. I. Norton, 'The Amount and Source of Millionaires' Wealth (Moderately) Predicts Their Happiness.' *Personality and Social Psychology Bulletin* 44(5) (May 2018): 684–699.

$10 million appear to be happier than others (as long as they earned the wealth themselves). And to earn such a significant amount of wealth, you usually have to be pretty remarkable in whatever field you are in.

Being exceptional generates both financial and emotional rewards. You should strive to be exceptional not only because you are good at what you do, but also because you want to be the very best at what you do. Being the best brings benefits like wealth, pride in yourself and your work, and general happiness. Being exceptional also gives you the positive feeling of knowing that you left a mark on the world. If your journey to excellence doesn't result in you becoming one of the very best in the world, you will still have achieved *your* possible best. And, along with that you will not only have happiness, satisfaction and material rewards, but you will also have the incomparable feeling of knowing that you gave it your all and left nothing to chance.

MAXIMIZE YOUR POTENTIAL

Most people, regardless of their age, can look back and think about how they could have made different choices or done things differently. When I was young, I didn't think about being the best I could be. I didn't have an awareness of what it meant to maximize my potential or be exceptional. I simply didn't think about it. And as I got older, my goals were to do reasonably well in every aspect of my life and to achieve balance—something I believe I have attained so far.

But I do wonder now: *Did I take away the potential for my children to become exceptional?* Could I have behaved differently as a parent to help vault my children into becoming world changers? Did I inadvertently inhibit their potential and their contributions to the world? I don't know. I am pleased with how my children's lives are playing out. My wife and I have always tried to be good parents, and our children are doing well in their lives and their careers, but I wonder if, as parents, we could have done things differently so that they maximized their potential and left an indelible mark on the world stage. As an example: Many exceptionals come from an environment where pursuing excellence and pushing the boundaries were always expected, not merely desired. I am not sure I set that expectation. Is our 'participation trophy' culture taking away the potential from our children to strive to become exceptional?

As I learned more about becoming exceptional, I realized that it means to fully maximize your potential to achieve your possible best, a concept I will discuss in more detail. Being your very best applies to everyone. It could be kids on a sports team or adults in business or a profession. Your stage of life does not matter; your state of mind does. This book is for you as long as your state of mind is about being the best you can be.

Excelling at something requires practice, repetition and volume, and this only happens with time. You have to log the hours to achieve a high degree of proficiency in anything. This is why the sooner you start, the better you can be. So, if you desire to become exceptional, you need to start today, because lost time is the only thing you cannot make up.

THE ELEMENTS
OF EXCELLENCE

INTRODUCTION

9.69 SECONDS

During the Beijing Olympics in the summer of 2008, the world fell in love with Usain Bolt, the fastest human the world has ever known. Bolt won the 100-meter final in an astonishing 9.69 seconds, shattering his previous world record time. He had a relatively slow start off the blocks but kept picking up speed and passing other runners as he raced. He was so far ahead that with 20 meters to go, he slowed down to savour his victory, well before the race was over. His 100-meter sprint is quite likely the most memorable performance in track-and-field.

How can someone be so extraordinary that while racing against seven of the fastest humans on earth, in a race that lasts less than 10 seconds, he has the time to slow down and celebrate even before reaching the finish line? Oh, and by the way, he was running with an untied shoelace.

In addition to smashing the world record in the 100-meter race in Beijing, Bolt also broke the world record in the 200-meter race, and then helped the Jamaican team win and set a new world record in the 4x100-meter relay. Thanks to his blazing speed, Bolt has become one of the most recognized athletes of our time. He has amassed eight Olympic gold medals, eleven world championships, and countless other medals and accolades that every other runner can only dream of.[1]

What made him exceptional? Was he born with a special gift, did he put in the 'requisite' 10,000 hours of deliberate practice, or did he have a level of determination and grit in him that others lack? Or was it something else?

Actually, it was a combination of all of these attributes and more that made Bolt exceptional. Most of the people who have achieved elite status in any field share the same characteristics that worked for Bolt. If you want to become exceptional or want to help your children or your team to consistently perform at their peak ability, you can employ the same set of attributes that have helped Bolt and the most outstanding and accomplished people in the world achieve their successes.

Bolt grew up in Sherwood Content, a small town in Jamaica where his parents ran the local grocery store. As a child, he did not dream of becoming a runner. All he wanted to do was play cricket, a sport he loved and played

---

[1]Usain Bolt did win a ninth gold medal in the 2008 4x100-meter relay but had to return it in 2017 after a teammate's positive drug test. Mather, Victor. 'Usain Bolt Stripped of Gold Medal After Relay Teammate Found Guilty of Doping.' *The New York Times*, 25 January 2017, www.nytimes. com/2017/01/25/sports/olympics/usain-bolt-jamaica-stripped-2008-olympic-relay-gold-medal-nesta-carter.html. Accessed on 1 August 2020.

well. His dreams were always about being part of the West Indies cricket squad and had he continued playing cricket, he very well may have been a formidable fast bowler and could potentially have helped his team to many world championships.

But he was born with a unique gift—speed—something that was apparent to everyone around him. In fact, it was his cricket coach who suggested he give track-and-field a try, which he did, and the rest, as they say, is history. Genetically, Bolt was built for generating speed. Speed is one of the physical attributes that can only be worked on and refined. It cannot be created. Either you are born with it, or you are not.

Speed is dictated by body shape, muscle length, strength and composition. The muscles of an average human consist of about 50 per cent fast-twitch and 50 per cent slow-twitch fibres. Slow-twitch fibres are efficient users of oxygen and help with muscle usage over longer periods of time. Fast-twitch fibres are the opposite and created for generating short bursts of speed or strength. The muscles of elite sprinters have more than 80 per cent fast-twitch fibres. If you are a sprinter, this is a gift. No matter how hard you work, you cannot convert slow-twitch fibres to the fast-twitch variety. You need to be born with enough of them to be an elite sprinter, as Bolt was.

Sprinting is less about the speed at which your legs move and more about the number of strides you take. Sprinters try to minimize the amount of time their foot is on the ground and generate maximum strength when they push off so that they cover more distance while their feet are in the air. In a typical 100-meter race, Bolt, aided by the leg length of his six-foot five-inch frame, takes about 41 strides to cover the distance. His competitors, all elite sprinters, take almost 45 strides, and that mismatch is hard to overcome.

The point here is that Bolt and all of the other most exceptional people were born with certain attributes that simply gave them an advantage over others who weren't born with them. It could be something obviously physical, such as speed or power or size. Or it could be exceptionally high intelligence, or an artistic ability or musical ability or anything else that serves as a natural gift certain people can build upon. If you read no further into this book, the first lesson to realize is that to become exceptional, you need to start in a domain where you have a natural strength, whatever it may be. With the right amount of effort, you can become good at just about anything, but trying to become exceptional in a field where you don't have a natural ability is simply an exercise in futility. We all have a talent or a gift; you just need to honestly determine what it is.

What you are born with is simply the start. Then there is everything else.

Usain Bolt happened to hail from Jamaica, a country where running is the most popular sport and a nation with a long tradition of nurturing many of the best sprinters in the world. Track stars are revered and everybody with an ounce of talent not only wants to be a sprinter, but dreams of being the best in the world.

To get a taste of the popularity of running in Jamaica, look no further than the event locally known as Champs, a track-and-field meet that is one of the most popular sporting events in the country. You could consider it equivalent to the Masters or the Super Bowl in the US.

Champs is not a professional meet with the best athletes and runners from around the world. It is the local high school tournament. With more than 3,000 students competing, Champs is the largest high school competition in the world. This is quite a statement for a country whose population is under three million people. For a Jamaican, winning a medal at Champs is akin to winning an Olympic medal.

The running culture is so strong in Jamaica that when Bolt was 15, he competed in the World Junior Championships, which happened to be in Kingston, Jamaica, his home. Bolt, getting ready to run on the biggest stage in his own country, was so nervous before his race that he put his shoes on the wrong feet. He won gold regardless, a victory that he still cherishes as one of his biggest moments.

Bolt became exceptional not only because he was born with a special gift, but also because he came from an environment and culture where running is nurtured. But this is only the start of what made him so special.

Bolt had an unmistakable self-belief, not only in knowing that the 100-meter distance was right for him, but a feeling where he truly believed he was ready to win a race. He had done the work, and at race time, there was no doubt in his mind he would emerge victorious. This inner confidence, or self-efficacy, is another trait shared by the most exceptional people in the world. Many Olympic races are lost before the starting gun goes off because some athletes don't believe they belong on that grand stage. Not so for Bolt. His unshakable self-belief helped him get the best out of his abilities.

Bolt's first Olympic appearance was at Athens in 2004, where after a lacklustre performance, partly due to a hamstring injury, he returned home empty-handed and disappointed. Shortly after his return, he started working with Glen Mills, the most respected track coach in Jamaica, whose athletes have collectively won over one hundred Olympic and world championship medals.

Mills saw the potential in Bolt but also saw weaknesses. He spent two years simply breaking the bad habits Bolt had developed that caused injuries and prevented him from fulfilling his potential. When Mills first started training Bolt, he noticed poor running mechanics. Specifically, he saw that Bolt ran behind his centre of balance (or with a slight back lean). This body position put pressure on his lower back, hips and eventually his hamstrings. Coach Mills wanted to fix the root cause of the problem and it all started with proper mechanics, which included a better running form facilitated by a slight forward lean.

As is true with most exceptionals, Bolt's success was largely influenced by his coach and mentor, who was able to help extract the full potential and talent that Bolt had within him. Every individual who has earned outstanding achievements, regardless of the field, can point to the specific people and mentors who helped them become the best. The journey to becoming elite is long, winding, rough and impossible to traverse alone.

One area in which Bolt and his mentor did not see eye to eye was the distances Bolt was best suited to run. Up until that point, Bolt hadn't been a 100-meter sprinter; he had competed in the 200-meter distance at the Athens Olympics, and his coach thought he could also be competitive as a 400-meter runner.

Many runners, including the great sprinter Michael Johnson, have specialized in the 200/400-meter combination. And while Coach Mills thought that Bolt's tall frame would lend itself better to the 400-meter distance, Bolt believed within himself that he could excel at the 100-meter sprint. Regardless of what anybody else believed, Bolt was committed to participating in the 100-meter race and becoming the fastest human in the world.

Eventually, his coach made a deal with him and said that he could compete in the 100-meter race only if he broke the Jamaican record for the 200-meter distance. Mills knew that this was a feat not likely to happen, as the Jamaican 200 record was set in 1971 and had remained unbroken for generations. Bolt, however, shattered that record at the 2007 Jamaican championships and finally ran in his first 100-meter race—just one year before he won in Beijing and became a household name as the fastest man ever.

To attain excellence, Bolt and Mills needed to work on the minutest of details, the microactions that would result in unmatched performance. Their goal was to get every minute detail right because you revert to your old and undesirable habits when you are under the intense pressure of a major race. As a result, Bolt had dedicated himself to refining and excelling in every little activity that gave him speed. He developed an improvement plan focused on those microactions, such as impact, stride length, centre of balance, head position and breathing. Each component had the potential to either shave off fractions of a fraction of a second or allow him to train harder and remain injury-free.

He broke up the 100 meters—a race that lasts less than 10 seconds—into chunks and had a strategy for each segment. He wanted to be 'tall' starting out of the blocks and to be able to look left and right at the 50-meter mark, and then during the final 10 meters, explode in a way that no one in the world could ever catch him. This *microexcellence*, or an extreme focus on the details, is what separates the great from those who are very good. There was never a plan B for Bolt. He was a runner, and that was that. Having running as his only path allowed him to concentrate on perfecting his skills and honing his physical abilities. By never even considering a safety net—a 'viable' career—Bolt not only excelled at his plan A but became the best ever at his craft.

Bolt certainly put in the hours of intense and hard work. Intensity, as well as the hours or volume of training, is irreplaceable. You don't put in the effort; you don't achieve the results. It's that simple. There is no shortcut, no matter how talented you are. Bolt's intense workouts and training regimen often had him lying on the track with exhaustion, only to get up again and do more repetitions of whatever he was working on at the time.

His outward reputation may have been that of a fun-loving, partying athlete who was born with immense talent, but the reality was that he trained for 11 months of the year, and his training was hard and strenuous. He would often be found sprinting in the hot Jamaican sun with a big belt around his waist, that held a strap dragging a stack of heavy weights on the track behind him as he ran, until he was past the stage of exhaustion. Over and over again. He knew he wanted to be the best in the world and saw from other runners as well as other athletes the effort required to become the best.

Bolt did not achieve greatness solely because he was born talented or put in the practice or worked hard or had grit and determination. It was all of that and more.

BECOMING EXCEPTIONAL

We have all been amazed by the achievements of a special set of incredibly gifted and talented individuals. In every field, there are people who have achieved a rare and elite status. Their talents and accomplishments are admired, envied and emulated.

These individuals have scaled the top of the pyramid and have reached seemingly unreachable heights. They may be athletes who have transcended to a single-name status, such as Tiger or Michael or Ronaldo, or they may be people you have never heard of at all who have invented lifesaving drugs or won the Nobel Prize by making fundamental advances in knowledge. Or they may have changed the world through science or music or business by influencing millions or perhaps billions of lives.

Each of these individuals is special, gifted and talented, and also hardworking, determined, persistent and lucky. They have each learned how to become the best and demonstrate their best work. They have come as close to maximizing their potential as possible.

The rest of us may have the same physical and mental attributes as many of these most extraordinary individuals. But there is something, a seemingly intangible set of traits, that separates the elite few from people who are accomplished, skilled and almost as good. This set of traits also separates them from the vast majority of people who possess the fundamental skills and talents to become exceptional but who often underappreciate and underutilize these qualities. In other words, they don't live up to their potential.

The difference between the elite few and everybody else is partly based on the traits and qualities they were born with or their environment—things outside their control. And it is partly based on the choices they make or sacrifices they are willing to endure. The qualities that make someone exceptional can be understood, developed and nurtured; in other words, you can give yourself the best chance of achieving excellence.

For most people, reaching the top of a particular field requires a transformational change in their attitudes, habits, beliefs and effort. Just picking out an area or two to incrementally improve upon will make you a little bit better, but it won't make you the best in the world. To become the best, you need to understand all the components, or building blocks, that are necessary for being the best. And then you must apply them to your life.

Becoming exceptional is possible for every person and every profession. No matter what you do, being at your possible best is the surest way to ensure success and have the satisfaction of knowing that you have given it your all and not left anything on the table.

In contrast, not attempting to become exceptional leads to inertia, declining satisfaction with your work, a listless attitude that affects you and those around you, a low sense of self-worth, a resentment of the success of others and a negative view of life that brings you down a spiral that's hard to get out of.

If you are reading this book, you want to become exceptional and achieve your possible best. Most people do. They want to be the best at their craft and are willing to put in the effort, but are just not sure how to do it. They often read articles and books that may have some very defined or prescriptive suggestions of steps to success, but these may not be relevant or applicable to everyone. Every exceptional has a different route to how they achieved mastery in their field, and your journey may be like no one else's. But every journey to the top shares a set of common elements, and adopting these elements in your life gives you the best chance to become exceptional in your field.

YOUR POSSIBLE BEST

We often talk about achieving our personal best. That is a backward-looking statement because it means that we are trying to do something better than we previously have. Being exceptional transcends the notion of personal best and brings us to achieving our *possible best*, a focus on maximizing what you can achieve rather than doing something a little better than you did the last time. Just thinking about your possible best instead of your personal best changes how you think about getting better. You stop taking a short-term view of incremental improvement, and instead, you take a longer-term transformational view of reconstruction. You begin to think about a total makeover of your attitude, your commitment, your goals and your effort, and you must improve each one of these qualities incrementally until they add up to the transformation you desire.

Whether or not your possible best results in the same level of outcome as the most gifted individuals, you need to push the boundaries of your own abilities and consistently strive to reach your own possible best. In some cases, it will result in you becoming the best in the world. In other cases, it will result in you being the best you can possibly become. Maybe it is becoming the most successful salesperson in your company, or maybe it is innovating and creating brand new value in the world. Maybe it's becoming CEO of the company you work for, or maybe it is reaching a certain level in music or sport or in your profession. Only when you maximize your potential and achieve your possible best do you have a chance of becoming exceptional.

Achieving your possible best means you have reached previously unreachable heights, are recognized for your outstanding accomplishments, and reap the rewards that go with being extraordinary in your field. When you aim to attain your possible best, you are thinking only about what you can accomplish. You are not thinking of bettering a mark you set earlier; you are not distracted by what other people are doing and how you fare relative to them. Your bull's-eye is what is possible for you and what can make you the best you can be. Focusing solely on this target provides clarity and instils a liberating feeling that frees you up and lets you reach your potential. This is how the most extraordinary people in the world have achieved their success.

The search for excellence is nothing new. We have always wanted to strive for excellence. I believe that we are biologically programmed to want to excel and do the best we possibly can. Most of us are smart, motivated and driven. And with the world of information just a click or a tap away, we have access to all the knowledge we need to become leaders in our fields. But the vast majority of us squander our opportunities and don't live up to our potential. In fact, only 2 per cent to 6 per cent of people actually achieve the goals and aspirations they set for themselves.

Most people simply end up giving up on their dreams and potential.

We don't achieve our potential for one of two reasons: First, we don't put the effort into it. We hope for something external to come in and make it happen for us, and invariably, the odds of an external force transforming us are about as high as the odds of any of us winning the Mega Millions lottery. Second, we don't know how to achieve our potential. We put the effort in, but the circumstances may not be right for us, or we focus on the wrong things or listen to the wrong advice or do things the wrong way and fail. And the reaction to failure is that we typically give up or try something else.

Very often, we can't even fathom what our possible best is. We view achieving extreme success as this faraway light in the sky reserved for other people and not us. We can see it, but we don't believe we can reach it, and even if we want to get there, we don't know how. There appears to be a massive space—a vacuum—between us and the light, and most of us are too intimidated to start the journey. Some start and falter, and some take the long circuitous route that gets them lost and very soon looking for another destination.

But it doesn't have to be that way. What if we knew the road that the most exceptional people have taken? That would certainly help us. It may not guarantee success, but it will certainly give us a map and a direction for our trek that makes that big elusive light more accessible.

IT IS NOT ONE SINGLE THING

Being the best in the world at something certainly requires natural abilities and talent, but that is not nearly enough. One popular theory suggests that 10,000 hours of deliberate practice is required to excel at something, but that too is insufficient. Being exceptional requires grit and perseverance and commitment. But individually, these also are not nearly enough. It also requires a high degree of emotional intelligence and a growth mindset, but again, these are not enough individually.

Being exceptional is multifaceted. It is a combination of innate abilities, intense effort and a set of enabling factors that make success possible, all rolled into one high-functioning package. The combination of these attributes is paramount, as each is required. Simplifying extraordinary performance to a single trait is naïve and misleading.

It would be nice to roll becoming exceptional into a single characteristic that we can all focus and work on, but as we may expect, there are multiple qualities necessary for becoming elite in any endeavour. If you want to achieve extreme success, you need to understand the breadth of attributes that drive extraordinary achievement and apply them to your life.

The exceptionals share a range of common factors, at either a conscious or subconscious level, and have used them to their fullest. Each of these factors, or elements of excellence, is essential for you to become exceptional in a world that is becoming more complex and in which standing out is more difficult than it has ever been in the past.

The surest way to achieve your possible best is to understand and apply the shared attributes that are present across the vast majority of journeys to excellence. Only then are you giving yourself the best chance of joining the ranks of the exceptionals. While your voyage may have its unique twists and turns, the set of essential conditions that you need remain unchanged.

There are two outcomes for you in applying the principles laid out in this book. The first is personal. You have the chance to be among the very best at something in the world, and when you do, you will have succeeded in achieving an unfathomable level of excellence that most people can't even dream about. The second is societal. Imagine if, as a human race, we could all attain a higher level of excellence, if we all operated closer to our possible best. We would solve more problems, eliminate more disease, create more significant breakthroughs, entertain more people with our athletic and artistic skills, and enhance societal value in every way.

And when more people become exceptional, all of our lives get better.

EXCEPTIONAL BUT NOT ALONE

Usain Bolt is truly extraordinary, the undisputed best of the best. He is the perfect combination of being born with natural talent, being nurtured in the right environment, having the right mental makeup, believing in himself, having the benefit of good mentoring, focusing on the right elements, committing fully to a goal, putting in the effort and making the right choices at the right times.

It was never a single thing that separated Bolt from everyone else and made him the greatest in his sport. It was always a combination of things. Anyone who says they have the magic bullet that can make you great just does not understand that it takes a spectrum of characteristics, like the ones Bolt exhibited through his incredible achievements.

Bolt is certainly not alone in how he became exceptional. The stories of the most exceptional people in the world are similar to his. Maybe other exceptionals have a bit more of one trait and a bit less of another. Still, by and large, the characteristics that made Bolt exceptional are the same ones that drive excellence in the most elite individuals and teams around the world in every domain. Understanding these characteristics and embracing them in your life can help you become extraordinary.

1

THE ELEMENTS OF EXCELLENCE

Wouldn't it be good if there was a formula for becoming exceptional? Can we create one equation that shows us the factors and elements required for sustained excellence? Specific traits made Michael Jordan, Tiger Woods, Bill Gates and Albert Einstein into the people they became. Is it possible to try and quantify these traits? Can we understand and analyse phenotypes of the most exceptional people and use them to build a model that we can use to replicate the degree of their achievements for ourselves or for our children?

When we understand how the most exceptional people became who they are, we see patterns emerge—common traits that all of them share. We may believe that remarkable individuals have a single characteristic that we can emulate. But if that were the case, depending on who you believe, all it would take is the right set of genes: You can achieve only based on whatever you're born with. Or it might simply take hard work—to the tune of 10,000 hours or more—

whether you have talent or not. We know that it isn't that simple. There isn't just one characteristic of Bill Gates that you can copy to become someone as exceptional as him. Even Gates himself would be unable to accurately list all of the traits—the multiple, interacting traits—that make him exceptional.

But in a general sense, there is enough data to know what goes into becoming exceptional. We can understand the essence of greatness and what it takes. Through years of research on exceptional individuals and performance, we can begin to form a picture of what is required to become the very best in any field. And yes, there is a formula that serves as a starting point for understanding what it will take to become exceptional.

The formula is quite simple: Fifty per cent of what it takes to become exceptional is genetic (the innate abilities you are born with). Twenty-five per cent comes from the intense effort and hard work you put in to improve your skills. The final 25 per cent comes from a set of enabling factors, or enablers, that drive success, including your environment, self-belief, ability to use knowledge to advantage, ability to focus on the minutest of details and your level of passion and commitment.

Let's examine each of these three components.

INNATE ABILITIES

To help us understand the role played by our genes, we have to thank all of the twins in the world. Twins have provided us with a real-world laboratory for determining how much of being exceptional is innate and how much is developed and influenced by our environment and other factors.

Identical twins share 100 per cent of their genes, which means that any difference between them must be due to external forces. If they grow up together, they also share much of the same environment: They share the same parents, home, nurturing, level of family education and wealth and many other conditions. So, we would naturally expect them to display very similar outcomes in their lives. If they grow up to become remarkably different in any way, we can say with a reasonable degree of certainty that whatever differences they exhibit are due to outside agents and influences.

In numerous studies on twins, conducted around the world, researchers have been able to link genetics with performance. In general, most of the twin studies tell us that what you are born with plays an outsized role in your performance across a range of activities and professions. Whether it is intelligence, body type, size or aerobic capacity, genetic traits account for the majority of variability in performance.

But talent and activity-specific skills are not the only things that are genetic. Even the factors that bring out a person's talent—motivation, desire and drive—are genetic to some degree, with some people just being born with a deeper drive and a more intense need to succeed than others. Some people are just more competitive or more tenacious by nature than others.

The impact of these *innate abilities* on performance has been studied across sports, music, language, mathematics, writing and other categories. Although no one can exactly quantify the amount of influence genes or DNA have on performance, the estimates of how much genes contribute to high performance are generally over 50 per cent. This means that innate abilities influence the exceptional achievements we observe more than any other factor—contributing to half or more of the effect.

Our whole lives, we have heard comparisons like, 'He gets his athleticism from his father' or 'She gets her smarts from her mother' or 'They are a musical family'. From the beginning of time, people have tried to make connections and find resemblances between certain traits and skills among members of families.

The power of shared genetic traits is real, and high-level skills and talents are no different. Skill is largely determined by your genes or your natural talent. You have to be born with the right markers that will make you successful in a domain. Everyone has natural talent in some area; your chances of success will depend on whether you find your innate skills and can take advantage of them. It can be intelligence, spatial ability, linguistic ability, musical ability or raw athletic attributes like power and speed. You can't attain excellence without these fundamental characteristics that largely come from your parents through your genetics. With the right level of effort, you can morph natural talent into world-class ability, but you cannot create something out of nothing. Understanding what you are truly gifted at is the first step towards being extraordinary at it. Every person who has reached an elite level in any field has done so by building on a natural ability. You will not become exceptional in a field in which you have limited innate talent.

However, it is important to keep in mind that natural talent serves only to separate approximately the top 10 per cent from everybody else. Distinguishing yourself within the top 10 per cent—reaching the 1 per cent or even the permyriad level—depends on how well you build on your natural talents.

INTENSE EFFORT

Although genetics is responsible for a large chunk of what it takes to become extraordinary, it is just the start. We can enhance or reduce the contribution of our natural talent by developing it further or letting it atrophy and waste away. Just because some of us inherit a unique gift from our parents does not always imply that we do something with it. Sometimes, we may not even know we possess a special talent that can be developed into world-class performance. To become exceptional is to start with natural ability and then put in the intense effort and invest the time and energy necessary to maximize the potential of our talents.

Skill development in any area is enhanced with practice and effort. Whether in music, sports, surgery, architecture, business or any other field, practice and skill development are required for exceptional outcomes. The connection between practice and performance varies across activities. It is higher and more directly observable for activities such as education, sports, or music, where you clearly see the impact effort and practice have on performance. Whereas other professions, such as business, law and medicine, have a more tenuous link between practice and outcomes, primarily because they are harder to measure.

But in all cases, deliberate skill development and practice—or quite simply hard work and intense effort—have a material impact on performance. As a general rule, and depending on the domain, up to 25 per cent of variance in exceptional performance can be attributed to hard work and practice.

To become exceptional, you need to have a highly refined set of skills in your field. In some cases, it is easy to determine who the best is because the results are objective and based on merit: You either win a race or a match, or jump higher than the rest. In other cases, who is best is determined subjectively, for example, with musical talent, gymnastics, business acumen, the ability to paint or to design a building. But regardless of how the best are judged, they are usually the ones with the most advanced set of skills in their domain.

The exceptionals hone their skills through intense effort and hard work and there is no substitute for volume of effort and serious and deliberate practice. Every single exceptional has worked incredibly hard and has devoted years, even decades, of their lives to getting better at their craft. No matter how gifted you are, you have to put in the work. Tiger Woods, one of the most gifted golfers ever and whose prodigious skills were on display on national TV when he was only two years old, reportedly worked on his game for 13 hours a day. Tennis star Novak Djokovic trained for 14 hours a day. While building Microsoft in the early years, Bill Gates never believed in the concept of taking weekends off and reportedly never took a vacation in his twenties. That is the sort of dedication and sacrifice required to join the permyriad.

The most common statement of an exceptional is, 'No one will outwork me.' Although we'll discuss a roadmap for how you can shatter barriers and become exceptional in your field, if you don't have the desire or the ability to put in the effort, you should understand that you will not reach the pinnacle of your profession. The good news is that as you start to see early successes and keep building on them, the work—although it will be gruelling—becomes easier as the level of motivation and passion for your activity increases.

ENABLERS

If, in general, natural abilities are responsible for 50 per cent of exceptional performance and intense effort accounts for another 25 per cent, there is still 25 per cent of unexplained variance. Just having the right genes and working hard will make you very good, but to become truly outstanding, you need a set of skills that enables your absolute best to emerge.

These missing pieces, collectively called *enablers*, include the following:

- The environment that shapes you
- The level of commitment you are able to maintain
- Your belief in yourself
- Your ability to take advantage of the world of information available to you
- Your ability to focus on the tiniest of details

These skills allow you to maximize your learning, growth and performance—and every exceptional individual possesses them.

These enabling skills bring out your talent and ensure your efforts are not misdirected. For example, your early environment significantly influences how you develop. If you are surrounded by smart, driven people who continually strive to achieve more, you will raise the bar for yourself. If the expectations around you are to excel at everything you do, then you are going to strive for exceptional performance all the time. If you are born into a family of musicians, your innate musical talents are more likely to be exposed, just as analytical skills would be more easily nurtured if you were born into a family of computer programmers or physical talents would be perceived and encouraged in a family that excels in a specific sport.

The exceptionals' desire to excel is so intense that most of us can't relate to it. The desire to become their possible best becomes a need, which is required to fuel the effort and commitment necessary to get to the pinnacle of a profession. Also, deep in their minds, they truly and deeply believe they are capable of performing at the highest level and have the confidence that they can rise to the top. This self-assuredness—the unwavering belief that they can be the best in their field—drives the most accomplished people to achieve their greatness.

Enabling skills also include an attitude of belonging. Many people may be just as good as the elite few but they don't believe they belong on the stage they are performing on. Tennis star John McEnroe's first Wimbledon appearance was as an 18-year-old amateur. His brilliant play that year led him to the semi-final match against the powerhouse Jimmy Connors. McEnroe lost that match in four sets. He believes he lost to Connors before he even walked onto the court. The atmosphere was simply too overwhelming for him to overcome, and he felt he didn't belong on that stage. Many Olympics races are won or lost before the gun goes off because the situation overwhelms the athlete. This is a feeling we can all relate to. Sometimes you falter in an important presentation or fail in some other significant activity for the very same reasons.

Very few people have the discipline and commitment to follow through on a single desire. Most of us get distracted or are drawn to other opportunities along the way and are unable to demonstrate the singular focus required to excel. The exceptionals share an unwavering commitment to the targets they set. Many of them have established precise and specific goals very early on. Björn Borg, the tennis ace who won five straight Wimbledon titles, had, as an eight-year-old, the specific goal of playing on Centre Court at Wimbledon. Like Borg, most exceptionals have similar pointed goals and set long-term targets at a very early stage in their development.

But what separates the exceptionals from everyone else is not just having such goals but possessing an unwavering commitment to achieving them that lasts years or decades. This level of commitment is one of the enabling skills you can learn to possess.

The exceptionals also understand the reality of the effort they need to make and are smart about learning. They understand that the body of knowledge required for excellence in any domain is vast and increasing, and they build an unmatched knowledge base not only of everything they need to know in their own field but by borrowing relevant ideas from other domains and other people. They have built a community of experts they can rely on for learning and support. This ability to manage the growing level of complexity required to become elite helps them improve at an accelerated pace. They know how to get better at getting better and as a result, the difference between the great and the good keeps getting larger until it becomes insurmountable.

The exceptionals know that they need the ability to call on their skills and expertise when it matters most. Regardless of your profession, you need to be able to peak at the time when peak performance is required. You can't be a great surgeon only in your mind; being an exceptional surgeon matters only when there is a patient, whose life depends on your skill, waiting on the operating room table. You can't be a great pianist when you practice; you become great by delivering outstanding performances. You can't break the world record during training; you can only be a great athlete if you perform your best at the big event.

Enabling skills are a collection of characteristics that are necessary to become elite in a field. They are all necessary to achieve the highest level of performance and can't be simplified into a single trait such as motivation, commitment, planning or grit. They need to be understood at an individual level. Any one of them can make a world of difference to your performance, so it is critical to understand how they apply to you.

VARIABLE CONTRIBUTION

Although the contribution of the three sets of skills varies from person to person and from profession to profession, a good starting point to understand the contribution of the three broad elements that make up exceptional performance can be summarized as follows:

- 50 per cent innate abilities
- 25 per cent intense effort
- 25 per cent enablers

A fine line separates those who reach the very top of their field from those who don't. While a significant amount of excellence is inborn, your innate skills are just the start and merely serve to place you in a position from which you can excel. At this point, your ability to put in the effort and your enabling skills take over and prove to be the differentiators between those who become exceptional and those who don't.

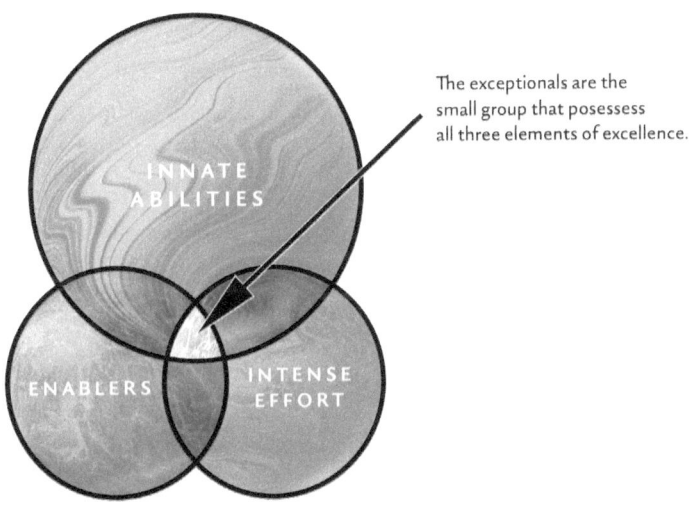

The exceptionals are the small group that posessess all three elements of excellence.

Figure 1.1. The three essential skill sets of exceptionals.

People who possess a single skill set (the vast majority of people in a single circle in figure 1.1) are average. They have some capabilities, but they don't really do anything with them. A smaller group of people are highly accomplished. These are successful people who lie at the intersection of two of the circles. They are competent and skilled at what they do and most people aspire to be like them. Then there are the exceptionals, the very small subset of people who lie at the intersection of all three circles. These are the most noteworthy individuals who have achieved remarkable feats.

Each of the three abilities is singularly powerful. Any one of the three can separate you from others and play an enormous role in enhancing your performance. But combine them, and you shatter any boundary and transform yourself to become the best of the best.

Although you need each of the three skill sets, you don't need them in the same dose. Picture a jar filled with marbles of three different colours, each colour representing one of the three elements of excellence (innate abilities, intense effort and enablers). The number of marbles of each colour is not important, but the total number of marbles is; it represents how good you are. The most exceptional people have a very large jar filled to the brim with marbles. The larger the jar you fill up, the more elite you are in your field. The only requirement is that all three colours are represented in your jar.

The reason the colours themselves are less important is that you can become exceptional in different ways. The formula is not 50-25-25 for everyone. Some people become exceptional because they are born with an inordinate amount of natural talent; others put in more work and effort to compensate for less inherent ability. Some have the right set of enablers to help compensate for a slight lack in the other two areas.

The important thing to remember is that you will not become exceptional with just one or two of the colours. You need all three. We have all heard stories about immensely gifted and talented people who have not lived up to their potential, and just as often, we have heard stories of highly dedicated and hardworking people who, despite their best efforts, simply don't have the natural ability to get them to an elite level.

The good news is that once you understand these three elements of excellence, you can apply them to your life. Now that you know the drivers of excellence and their relative contributions, you have the formula to begin.

INNATE ABILITIES

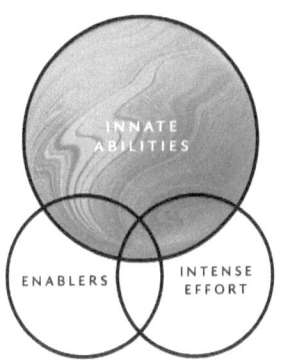

2

START WITH YOUR NATURAL TALENT

Norwegian chess prodigy Magnus Carlsen sat blindfolded, facing away from the tables. Behind him were 10 opponents sitting in front of their chessboards, ready to make their moves. None of them were blindfolded. The game was simple: Carlsen was supposed to play 10 separate games against these 10 opponents simultaneously. Being blindfolded, he was unable to see any board or opponent. Using standard chess notation, a moderator called out the moves each challenger played and Carlsen verbally replied with his counter. For example, the moderator would say something like, 'Board 2 played knight e7,' and Carlsen would respond with, 'Board 2, queen d2'. The moderator would then move on to Board 3. This would go on and on for every board and every move.[2]

---

[2]'Magnus Carlsen—Blindfold at Harvard University.' 2016, *YouTube*, https://www.youtube. com/watch?v=w1Rr4Uq1R-I. Accessed on 1 August 2020.

Carlsen had to mentally keep track of 10 separate games and the positions of 320 pieces on 640 squares. In a single chess game, the total number of possible combinations is so vast that attempting to count them is futile. By some estimates, there are more possible moves in a game of chess than the number of atoms in the known universe. Multiply that by 10 games, and you are just around the corner from infinity. When you add in the complexity of doing this without looking at a single board, the feat becomes an example of extreme human ability.

Carlsen won all 10 games.

To be fair, blindfold chess is not uncommon for the best players in the world. They practice playing blindfolded to be able to better visualize in their minds the board, moves and positions. Many excel at blindfold chess, and while not quite the parlour trick for the best players in the world, playing blindfolded against people of lesser abilities is easier than playing a regular chess match against players with equal skill. But blindfold chess still requires an incredibly gifted, rare, and disciplined mind.

There is no doubt that Magnus Carlsen is an exceptional talent, and his chess resume is unparalleled. A grandmaster at the age of 13, Carlsen went on to become the youngest-ever world number one when he was 19. He has achieved just about every accolade you can in chess, including the highest rating ever attained. While only in his 20s, he was already regarded as the greatest chess player of all time.

Carlsen was able to do this because of a rare and gifted

ability to see pieces, patterns and moves on a chessboard 'in the blink of an eye,' whereas others simply see chaos. This ability to create maps of potential chessboard moves is an innate skill and something that he believes happened automatically.[3]

From a very young age, he exhibited high intelligence and a unique ability to solve problems, jigsaw puzzles and advanced Lego structures, and would patiently spend hours working on them. He also had a keen sense for analysing patterns. His parents thought that the highly developed analytical skills he showed at an early age would lend themselves well to the game of chess. Carlsen was five when his father introduced him to chess in a way that made the game fun and accessible for his age. And while his father was a good player in his own right, chess was simply a fun family activity, making Carlsen's early experience with chess a positive one.

Over the years, his development was largely due to a single-minded focus, effort and dedication to chess, and the determination to become the best player in the world. But it all started with his pursuing an activity that built upon his natural talent and gifts. His skills in solving puzzles, thinking logically, spatially and analytically and patiently working through problems were transferable to chess. He was also fortunate enough to be encouraged to develop as a chess player and specialize in the game at an early age.

---

[3]'Magnus explains how his mind works from *Magnus* (2016).' *YouTube*, https://www.youtube. com/watch?v=IuAPVphOX4c. Accessed on 1 August 2020.

Growing up, he also enjoyed playing soccer, and perhaps if he had been encouraged to excel at soccer, the world might never have seen his chess talent emerge.

There are specific traits that all of us simply start with. Intelligence is one of them. It can be enhanced, advanced and nurtured, but a significant portion of your intellect is genetic. By many estimates, more than 50 per cent and sometimes up to 80 per cent of our variability in intelligence can be attributed to genes.

This outsized influence of your genetics is not just reserved for intelligence. Genetics or heritable traits are closely related to abilities across a wide range of areas. The high degree of genetic factors which contribute to outstanding skills in music, writing, mathematics, sports, memory and knowledge suggests that what you are born with plays a significant role in how good you become at something.[4]

To be very good at music, you need to have a discriminating sense of rhythm and hearing. This is something you either possess from birth or you don't. To be outstanding at tennis, golf and many other sports, you need to have the ability to generate power—again, something you are either born with or you aren't. If you want to be a sprinter, you need to be born with explosive speed, and to be a chess grandmaster, you need to have a high intelligence and an innate ability for analysis and strategy.

[4]Anna A.E. Vinkhuyzen et al., 'The Heritability of Aptitude and Exceptional Talent across Different Domains in Adolescents and Young Adults.' *Behavior Genetics* 39(4) (2009): 380–392, doi: 10.1007/s10519-009-9260-5.

To understand the power your genes and your DNA wield on your daily habits, look no further than popular genetic testing services such as 23andMe which are available to everybody. All you do in these tests is spit into a small tube and send the saliva sample to the company. Within a few weeks, you receive a detailed report of your ancestry, health and other traits. Your report not only includes whether you share the same gene variant as elite athletes, but even things like the ice cream flavours you are likely to prefer, whether you fear public speaking, your ability to match musical pitch, your ability to detect the odour of asparagus and even if you are likely to be afraid of heights. All of these traits and countless more are based on characteristics you are born with. It should come as no surprise then that your innate abilities play an outsized role in every outcome of your life.

So, what does this mean in a practical sense? How does this get you on the path to becoming exceptional?

This simply means that your first step toward being exceptional is to start in an area where you have a natural ability. Many people overlook this. We often strive toward an arbitrarily set goal for ourselves. Or we indiscriminately set goals for our children or co-workers without honestly evaluating if the domain we want to see excellence in matches their natural abilities and skills.

Parents especially want their children to excel at something and they tend to push them into areas they believe are right for them. While they are often correct, they often are not. They are perhaps projecting their unfulfilled desires onto their children. Magnus Carlsen's parents encouraged their five-year-old to learn chess because of the qualities they saw in him, and that is a lesson most parents would do well to learn.

One common element of the exceptionals is that they knew very early on that they were good at something. Matching your aptitude to the activities you wish to excel at is the starting point of becoming exceptional. Aptitude is foundational. Everything else is built on it.

APTITUDE CAN BE MYSTERIOUS

While you may not know what your natural abilities are, you tend to find out early on what you're *not* good at. Gandhi, one of the most exceptional people the world has ever known, studied law. However, he was not particularly good at practicing law. He froze in court during his first cross-examination due to the trouble he had managing the stress and anxiety of being in a courtroom.

Once Gandhi was exposed to social injustice, however, he quickly learned that his aptitude was in being a civil rights leader. He had the desire, skill and knack to influence people and facilitate change on a grand scale. The rest of his achievements are forever rooted in history.

If you are fortunate, then you may have discovered your true talents at an early age, as Carlsen did. Most people, though, fail to recognize their natural ability. But you have to trust that it will show itself—that it will become a pivot point or a flash of insight that exposes a unique ability that you must seize. Usually, it is the thing that comes easier to you than it does to other people around you. Or it could be something you did where you were surprised by how well you did it. And if you still can't recognize it, ask the people who are closest to you for an honest assessment of what they think your natural skills are. Make a list of things that come easiest to you and add to that what the people closest to you think your inherent skills are. If you are unsure of your natural abilities; this list will serve as a good place to start.

When you recognize your gift and it manifests itself in a profession that you can pursue, then you can start down the journey toward becoming exceptional. However, if you start in an area that is misaligned with your natural ability, then it is difficult to reach the top of your field.

Through hard work, grit and perseverance, you could have a successful career in an area that does not mesh with your natural aptitude. But it is your natural aptitude blended with these other factors that turn success into an exceptional outcome. It is this combination that advances you from good to great and from outstanding to elite. Take your time to determine what you are truly good at and keep in mind that what you are good at could very likely be different from what you enjoy or are passionate about. This is a common mistake people make. Your goal is to understand the areas where you have a starting advantage and not to find the areas you enjoy, although it certainly helps when both are the same.

UNDERSTANDING YOUR ABILITIES

Ask yourself, 'What am I truly gifted at?' If you can't identify your innate skills or you are in a career or vocation misaligned with your natural strengths, you will have a hard time excelling at it and stand the risk of being average or mediocre. Mediocrity leads to a lifetime of dissatisfaction for many people because they are unable to achieve their aspirations despite their best efforts.

When you don't have innate abilities in your profession, you miss out on one of the three core elements of excellence. You are only left with the other two: intense effort and enablers. These can get you a long way, and you can be successful in your field, but the best you can do with two of the three essential skills is become good, never great.

Fortunately, there are methods that you can use to understand your natural talents. Earlier, I had mentioned thinking about what comes most naturally to you or to ask those closest to you for their thoughts if you're unable to come up with your set of talents. You can also think about how you liked to spend your time when you were very young. At an early age, you were likely to migrate to the activities where you had a natural tendency to shine.

When I was young, I loved learning and reading and would read books endlessly, for hours and days, pretty much through my entire summer vacations. I never thought about being an author when I grew up and I wasn't one for the majority of my professional career. But now, having transitioned into an author, I can make the connection between my natural linguistic ability and my current vocation.

Each of us is born with a different set of abilities and 'intelligences or things we are innately better at than others. Some people are naturally good with space and directions; I'm not (a fact my wife will readily attest to). Some people have good hand-eye coordination, whereas others may have an inborn sense of rhythm or the ability to analyse patterns. Our brains are not all wired the same way and each of us is born with distinct capabilities that determine our eventual performance.

Noted Harvard psychologist Howard Gardner, creator of the multiple intelligence framework, makes an analogy of human abilities to multiple computers. He believes we are all born with multiple intelligences. A single form of intelligence shared by everyone is akin to the human brain acting as a single computer, where any variances in performance among different people are determined by how this one computer is programmed and developed.[5]

On the other hand, Gardner's research suggests that we are born with eight distinct types of intelligences—or eight different, independently programmed computers, starting from birth. How well you do at one of the eight intelligences does not necessarily influence the performance of the others. You simply start stronger in certain intelligences versus the others.

---

[5]'A Beginner's Guide to the Theory of Multiple Intelligence.' *MI Oasis*, https://www.multipleintelligencesoasis.org/a-beginners-guide-to-mi. Accessed on 1 August 2020.

This means that each human has a different set of skills that can be developed independently. The eight intelligences identified by Gardner are described in the following list. As you read, ask yourself which ones are your strengths.[6]

Spatial Intelligence

This connotes the ability to think abstractly and in multiple dimensions, and the capacity for spatial reasoning and spatial conceptualization. It is required for fields like architecture, graphic design, photography and fashion.

Bodily kinaesthetic intelligence

This is the ability to use your body in a way that demonstrates physical and athletic prowess. If you have this ability, you could be an athlete effortlessly running down a field or flawlessly handling a ball, or a dancer expertly performing a complicated routine.

Musical Intelligence

As the name suggests, this is the capacity to have an inherent understanding and sensitivity to rhythm, sounds, pitch, melody and other musical elements. The best musicians, composers, conductors, directors and songwriters have well-developed musical intelligence.

---

[6]The Components of MI.' *MI Oasis*, https://www.multipleintelligencesoasis. org/the-compo-nents-of-mi. Accessed on 1 August 2020.

Linguistic Intelligence

This is the ability to appreciate words and language and the ability to use words to communicate effectively when speaking and writing. The best writers and journalists require linguistic intelligence.

Logical-mathematical Intelligence

This indicates the ability to intuitively understand mathematical concepts, logical problems and the interrelationship between abstract concepts. The best computer programmers, mathematicians, physicists, economists, accountants, etc. share these characteristics.

Interpersonal Intelligence

This is to have well-developed social and emotional intelligence or the ability to understand and relate to people around you and be sensitive and appreciative of their unique styles. Leaders, negotiators, politicians and coaches share this trait.

Intrapersonal Intelligence

This is the ability to understand and be sensitive to your own thoughts and feelings and make personal decisions that align with your traits and desires. Primarily, it is to know and be in touch with yourself. While specific vocations such as philosophy or psychology may require this trait, according to Gardner, this skill is essential for everyone to be successful in our complex modern society.

Naturalistic Intelligence

This is the ability to understand the nuances in nature, including the distinction between plants, animals and other elements of nature and life. Success as geologists, botanists, farmers, biologists and other similar professions require this ability.

Each individual has a unique map of these eight abilities, with a more refined capacity in some abilities over others. If you review this list of eight intelligences, you likely know where your natural strengths lie. Write down traits within yourself that fit each intelligence type and score yourself on a scale from 1 to 10 for each of these abilities. Identify the intelligence where you have the highest score. Is the area in which you wish to excel in line with your natural intelligence or unique gift?

Of the thousands of careers, activities and vocations that you can participate in, each of them will relate to one or more of Gardner's intelligences. This list serves as a starting point to match your activities to your natural abilities.

THE RIGHT APTITUDE MARKERS ARE KEY

Gardner's eight intelligences serve as aptitude markers or the qualities that help you determine your unique strengths. You need to understand how these markers predict your ability to become exceptional in a profession. For example, even though the best surgeons require manual dexterity and visuospatial ability to operate on your body with zero errors, being strong in these abilities does not necessarily predict better surgeons.

Instead, personality traits and decision-making ability are higher predictors of success as a surgeon. Just because you can work well with your hands does not necessarily mean you have an aptitude for surgery. A lot more goes into being an exceptional surgeon than the ability to wield a scalpel expertly.

DOUBLE DOWN ON YOUR STRENGTHS

Reaching the very top of your field requires an increasing spiral of skill development, which is why it is vital to start building from the earliest set of skills you possess, which are your natural abilities. The earlier you start, the better your chances of extraordinary skill development, and the later you start, the harder it is to attain mastery of a skill.

It is essential to build on your natural abilities because skills beget advanced skills. Building on existing strengths produces a disproportionate increase in the output of subsequent skill-building efforts. For example, if you are learning a brand-new skill, one unit of effort may result in one unit of improvement. But if you are improving on a capability you already possess, one unit of effort will result in more than one unit of improvement. In other words, you get the biggest bang for the buck by investing in developing the skills you already have. No doubt enhancing weak areas is essential too, and if you lack the fundamental skills that are required to be successful in your field, then you have to get better at them. But that should never come at the expense of strengthening your strengths.

Every activity or profession is multidimensional, with specific areas or segments that require a high degree of competency. To become exceptional in your field, you need to have a strong skill set in each area. This means that you have to be at least in the top 10 per cent of your peer group in each category. In addition, you need to excel in one or maybe two areas—these become your differentiators or areas of strength. For these, you need to be in the top 1 per cent.

Improving your abilities from the top 10 per cent to the top 1 per cent in your area of strength plays a more significant role in exceptional performance than improving from being average to the top 10 per cent in your area of weakness (relative to your peers).

Professional golfer Rory McIlroy, who has ranked number one in the world, does as well or better than his peers in most statistical categories. But, in one aspect of the game—driving the ball off the tee—he dominates over others; this is his area of strength. We know this to be true because of the meticulous recording of golfing statistics, but this condition of dominating in a particular strength area is valid across all disciplines. Steve Jobs was highly competent at many tasks of managing a large and complex enterprise, but he was especially outstanding as a creative genius and innovator. The Beatles were very good across the range of skills necessary to become the most popular band in the world, but they particularly excelled as singers and songwriters.

Most exceptional people have one or two strengths that stand out relative to their peers and other areas where they are on par. So, when you find your specific area of strength, hone it until your skill in it clearly stands out and no one can come close to you in that particular activity. You will still need to work on all aspects of your domain, so you are not substandard in any area, but focusing on making your strengths stronger will go a long way.

As you discover what you are inherently gifted at and what you aren't, you need to ensure that you become reasonably good at your weaknesses, and if you can transform them into assets, that is fantastic and is a necessary step in your journey to excellence. But knowing and working on your strengths, whatever they may be, is what is going to separate you from everyone else and make you the best of the best.

NATURE BEFORE NURTURE

The eternal question of whether geniuses are born or made has been debated millions of times. The ancient Greek philosopher Plato believed human abilities were attributed to nature. In contrast, his most famous student, Aristotle, was of the opinion that the talents we develop come through nurture. And though it has been discussed endlessly throughout the subsequent millennia, no one has ever been able to answer the question satisfactorily.

Countless scholars and books push the virtue of natural ability and propose that the abilities you are born with are the primary determinants of what you achieve. Conversely, just as many intellectuals argue the opposite. They state that what you are born with has little impact on your achievements and some even believe you can take just about any new-born baby and develop them into becoming whatever you want because every skill is a learned skill.

The nature versus nurture debate is an outdated concept. Nature and nurture are both essential in extraordinary skill development. Genes may be predetermined but the environment shapes the characteristics they convey. Nature and nurture work together to form your progress, abilities and the heights you are capable of achieving.

Rather than try to pinpoint the origin of excellence, we need to focus on the methods to create it. And the process is simple: You start in an area where you have a set of skills or a natural gift and then you support that gift and invest in it until you have developed it into an extraordinary ability. That is how every exceptional has done it and it is the only way you can do it too.

APTITUDE IS ONLY THE START

We have all seen and heard stories about child prodigies or people who display early sparks of brilliance and who we believe are going to be world changers as their talents mature.

We think we are witnessing the great leaders, athletes, violinists or scientists of the future, only to see them burn out early and never fulfil their potential. While these prodigies may have displayed natural aptitude, we need to remember that aptitude is only the start.

Just because some people are precocious in a field does not mean that they will become exceptional at it. So much more is involved in developing skills, abilities and talent, that precociousness is nothing more than a modest indicator of potential. Natural talent needs to be nurtured and requires an environment that offers it the best chance to thrive. Aptitude needs significant investment, not only from the future superstars but from the people around them as well.

Of course, a natural skill set is crucial; without it, achieving excellence is elusive. But aptitude is by no means the only factor that drives success. For example, Magnus Carlsen had parents who saw his talents early and encouraged their growth. But that was only the start. He was focused on studying the game, he put in the hours—and years—of training, and he believed in his abilities.

You need all of these pieces to build your puzzle of excellence, but first you need to know what picture it will form. Where do your own special talents lie? Are you able to link the area you wish to excel in to your natural talents and abilities? If you exhibit natural talent in your domain, you are on the right path and already halfway toward your destination of becoming exceptional. The subsequent chapters in this book discuss how to traverse the second half of the journey.

THE ENABLERS

INNATE
ABILITIES

ENABLERS

INTENSE
EFFORT

3

REFINE YOUR ENVIRONMENT

Hungarian psychologist László Polgár had an idea about creating geniuses. After studying the lives of hundreds of brilliant intellectuals throughout history, he found that they all shared a common theme: early specialization and intensive training. Polgár believed that you could create a genius with just about any healthy child if they were influenced by the right environment and conditions.[7] He was so determined to prove his theories that he dreamed up the ultimate experiment—he would make his own children geniuses. But first, he had to get married and have children.

As he worked on his idea in 1965, he began writing to the woman who would eventually become his wife, Klára, describing the project he had in mind. He shared his

---

[7]Carlin Flora, 'The Grandmaster Experiment.' *Psychology Today*, 1 July 2005, https://www. psychologytoday.com/us/articles/200507/the-grandmaster-experiment. Accessed on 1 August 2020.

hypotheses around the notion that with early and intensive specialization, they would be able to create prodigies. He explained to her that he needed a wife who would work with him to try to prove his theory. She agreed to participate in his experiment and the couple got married and had three daughters.

As planned, the Polgárs created a setting where their children could learn and excel. All the couple knew was that they wanted to develop geniuses; they did not even know in which field. They considered mathematics, languages and other areas but eventually settled on chess when their oldest daughter, Susan, who was four years old, stumbled upon a chessboard in a drawer.

Chess seemed to be the perfect choice for this grand experiment. Success and proficiency in chess are entirely dependent on ability and merit; it is gender-neutral (even though men and women played in different tournaments at the time), the results are objective and performance is measurable.

László and Klára Polgár manufactured an environment for their daughters to excel at chess. They home-schooled their children in the family's modest apartment in Hungary. The girls spent between five and eight hours a day working on their chess skills and had dedicated time for learning languages, mathematics and a few other subjects. Their days were regimented not only with time for chess and studies, but with time set aside for table tennis, swimming and even a designated 20-minute slot for jokes.

Their apartment was packed with countless books on

chess and filled with the results and analyses of previous tournaments. Pictures of historical chess scenes adorned the walls of their home. The environment the girls grew up in was all about chess. It was designed to create an expectation of excellence in the game.

Only six months after Susan started learning chess, she was beating adults at local chess clubs. At 15, she became the top-ranked female player in the world and eventually the third woman in the world to attain the title of grandmaster. Her younger sister Sophia became an exceptional chess player as well, winning tournaments around the world, and her occasional losses in matches came against Susan.

And if the accomplishments of these two sisters are not impressive enough, the youngest, Judit, went on to have one of the most celebrated careers ever and is widely considered the best female chess player in history. She was the number one female player from 1989 to 2005, and at 15, had become the youngest grandmaster (at the time) in the game.

Not only did all three sisters become exceptional in their field (chess), but the experiment worked in every way. They grew up to become balanced and well-rounded individuals as well. They are smart, personable, articulate and friendly, and you can read about them or watch some of their videos on YouTube and judge for yourself.

There is a lot written about the Polgár sisters and their parents' experiment is truly fascinating. But, quite simply, what this story tells us is that three girls, growing up together within an environment created for excellence and supplemented with early specialization, intense training and practice, could all reach the very top of their field. Whatever conditions László and Klára Polgár established, they were effective in creating three of the most extraordinary chess players the world has seen.

SPECIALIZE EARLY

Like the Polgárs, the most exceptional people in the world have invested a lifetime of effort into becoming the best of the best at their specialty. Excellence comes from repeatedly spending time honing a set of skills. Since time is a fixed and finite variable, you need to start as early as possible to maximize the volume of effort you put into skill development. There are significant benefits to specializing and focusing on a single field.

Parents often face the question of how to allocate their children's time when the children show promise in a particular activity. Should they encourage their children to specialize in that specific activity at an early age or should they expose them to many different activities to help them become well rounded? Most parents take the latter path: They enrol their kids in piano lessons and sign them up for baseball, golf and soccer, plus maybe have them join a chess club, math club and coding camp—all designed to expose their kids to a wide array of activities. But while this approach may help them become jacks-of-all-trades, it also leads to them becoming the master of none.

Early exposure to a range of activities is a good thing. How else will you know what you are gifted at and where your interests, natural talents and abilities lie? Finding your gift is essential, because, as we have discussed, your best chance of reaching the most elite level in any field is by building on your natural talent. Talent is the one thing that cannot be taught; the skills to nurture it can.

However, once you have picked the activity where you can build on your natural talent and you have a desire to become exceptional at it, you have reached the point where you need to specialize.

Specialization is the deliberate, dedicated and structured focus on a single activity to the exclusion of other activities. It means a focus on being very good at only one thing, not being marginally good at several. It does not mean you give up doing other things, perhaps for fun and enjoyment or even to develop additional skills. It merely means you have picked the activity you want to excel in and are committed to putting in the effort required to become as proficient as possible at it.

The reason for specialization is simple. You can never replace the amount of time you need to dedicate to an activity. You need time to acquire and develop the necessary skills. The earlier you learn the basic skills, the sooner you progress to more advanced skills. The sooner you develop the advanced skills, the quicker you will develop best-in-class skills. And the quicker you gain best-in-class skills, the more likely you are to attain a rare and elite level of proficiency in your field that makes you among the best in the world.

Andre Agassi started to play tennis when he was four years old. By the time he was 17, he was competing against the best players in the world. His opponents, often in their late 20s, were in the prime of their careers. Agassi could keep up with them despite his youth because he had specialized in tennis at an early age and had built the same volume of practice on the court as players a decade older and he could compete against anyone. Through early specialization, Agassi gained the ability to go toe-to-toe against the best in the world. Playing against the best further refined his skills, until eventually, he became the top-ranked player in the world.

Early specialization in an activity is not something that is reserved only for future world champions, though. It is increasingly necessary even if you want your children to get a good education from a top university. The most elite universities are moving away from admitting well-rounded students who show moderate proficiency in many different things. They are increasingly looking for students who have demonstrated outstanding ability in one or two areas. They are looking for students who are superstars, not generalists. They no longer want to create classrooms filled with well-rounded students; they want to develop well-rounded classes, assembled with students who are exceptional in different fields.

The age at which you specialize depends on the activity you pick. Early specialization works particularly well for domains where the outcome depends primarily on specific skills honed through repetition, such as tennis, golf, chess, piano, writing computer code, running, cycling, figure skating, gymnastics, spelling and so many others. These activities require you to build specific muscles, techniques and skills.

For domains where skills are transferrable or for those that require a core foundational knowledge base, early specialization takes on a different form. You don't become an exceptional architect, physicist, surgeon, patent attorney or consultant by specializing in these professions as a youth. But just because no one becomes a patent attorney when they are 12 years old doesn't mean they weren't specializing. As youths, they were likely to have been building the essential ability to read and absorb vast amounts of information, one of the qualities that distinguishes good patent attorneys from great ones. These professions need not just domain-specific knowledge but foundational skills and knowledge that come from years and often decades of intense practice. Once you have the foundation, it is the specialization and development of task-specific skills that ultimately make you elite in your field.

Specialization alone will not make you exceptional. It is one of several attributes required for attaining excellence—necessary but not sufficient, which means that merely specializing in something will not make you an expert. As we have already discussed, you also need to have natural talent or aptitude and the ability to put in the required effort. Moreover, you need to possess the set of enabling factors, such as the self-belief, confidence and ability to be fully committed to your goals to reach the very top of your field.

As a general rule of thumb, to become exceptional, you need to specialize as early as possible and practice, practice, practice. The most exceptional people have the clarity and vision to know what they want to achieve; they specialize in it and focus on becoming the best at it and are undaunted by the effort and work required.

YOUR ENVIRONMENT

Your environment includes the physical surroundings you find yourself in, the social environment of the culture and expectations placed on you, and even the characteristics and abilities of people around you who influence you daily. Everyone, whether it is a renowned scientist who pushes the boundaries of knowledge every day or an Olympic athlete who pushes the edges of human physical achievement, has been shaped, in large part, by an environment that supported their growth and development.

Your Physical Environment

To excel at anything, the first and most obvious need is to have unfettered access to the resources necessary—facilities, people and ideas—to make you successful. At the most basic level, if you want to become an exceptional skier, you need to have easy access to snow; if you're going to find the cure for a rare disease, you need ready access to a well-equipped lab. Physical facilities are just the beginning. You need access to training and mentoring, the ability to interact with and learn from your peers and sometimes, depending on your activity, the ability to match up your skill set against others.

As a result, talent thrives in hubs or localized areas. It happens when like-minded people interact and demonstrate their skills, and ideas clash and get refined—the clustering of talent results in raising the overall capabilities of the talent hub. Consequently, the best that emerge from these clusters are genuinely remarkable.

Clustering of talent leads to excellence in every field. The University of Chicago has the largest concentration of Nobel Prize–winning economists. Similarly, the most significant advances in medicine happen in specialized regions with world-class medical centres, such as Boston, home to the largest set of Nobel laureates in physiology and medicine. It is the collection of like-minded people and resources and infrastructure that lets talent develop and become exceptional.

In the US, places like Silicon Valley and Seattle create and attract the top technologists in the world and are home to the most exceptional tech talent and entrepreneurs. If you believe technology is the domain you want to excel in, your best bet is to be there. Jupiter, a little town in Florida with a population of 64,000, is home to more than 50 of the world's top golfers, and Rift Valley in Kenya is home to the highest concentration of the world's great marathoners.[8]

[8]Dylan Dethier, 'Home, Sweet Home: How Jupiter, Florida, Became the Epicenter of Professional Golf.' *Golf*, 12 February 2018, https://golf.com/news/home-sweet-home-how-ju-   piter-florida-became-the-epicenter-of-

The culture of running is so influential in Rift Valley that just about everyone who lives there personally knows some elite runners. When they see people they know shine at the world stage, they are motivated to lace up their own sneakers and take up running and try to excel at it, raising the collective bar of the region until the best in the world emerge.

World-renowned French horn player and teacher Julie Landsman is no stranger to exceptional performances from herself or her students. She credits the environment she grew up in for enabling her many successes as a musician, teacher and judge around the world. She benefited from the fact that she grew up very close to New York City and attended a high school that had a great band. Easy access to the city afforded her the luxury of access to high-quality performances and the ability to learn under an accomplished instructor who worked at the Metropolitan Opera. She was able to hear her teacher perform five times a week. The confluence of these environmental factors played a significant role in her success.

As you work on building your skills, you need to ask yourself if you are in supportive surroundings. Are the conditions around you such that they enable you to deliver

professional-golf/#:~:text=Officially%2C%2035%20 PGA%20Tour%20 pros,Rory%20McIlroy%20and%20Rickie%20Fowler. Accessed on 1 August 2020.; Faith Karimi and Idris Mukhtar, 'The Reasons Why Kenyans Always Win Marathons Lie in One Region.' *CNN*, 6 November 2019, https://www.cnn.com/2019/11/06/africa/ken-ya-runners-win-marathons-trnd/index.html. Accessed on 1 August 2020.

your best work? If your surroundings are not conducive for you to excel, you have to find the right environment where your abilities are pushed and your talents are exposed.

Keep in mind that your surroundings are always changing and that you need to learn how to excel under different conditions. For example, we are living through a time where remote work is replacing physical proximity in many jobs and professions. You need to ensure that the core benefits of being in a supportive physical environment don't go away.

The children born in present times may never see flying cars, but they will almost certainly be exposed to distance learning from remote universities. How they learn and excel will have to change. Students in medical colleges will have to excel at treating patients and collaborating with other physicians from afar; they will have to learn new ways to excel. But the fundamental impact of the role of the physical environment in the development of excellence will always remain.

Your Social Environment

You need an environment that not only affords you access to the physical facilities, tools and equipment you need, but also facilitates interactions with peers and gives you the ability to learn, exchange ideas and size up your skills. Your social surroundings play a critical role in how you develop extraordinary talent. Many of the exceptionals came from homes where discipline was valued, as was the need to work hard. Most important, they were steeped in a culture where high achievement and excellence were expected.

People tend to rise to the level of the expectations placed on them and the level of skill they witness around them. If you are in an environment where expectations are high, you will perform at a higher level. When you are exposed to situations where excellence is expected, you will very likely deliver it. And when you believe the most accomplished people are not too different from you, you think you also can achieve the same heights as them.

Juli Benson was an outstanding collegiate runner. But she wasn't Olympic calibre. Her times and performances were good for a university athlete but did not warrant an invitation to the Olympic trials. However, she still attended the 1992 Olympic trials—only as a spectator and not as a participant as she had hoped.

Simply being at the trials, in an environment surrounded by the best athletes in the country, sparked a fire in her. She began to believe she also belonged on that stage. As the announcers introduced each runner and the accolades they had achieved, she became more determined. She heard the names of people she knew. She believed that if they could do it, she could as well. Being present in that setting started to melt away the mental barriers that separated her from the Olympics and she began to feel like she could develop what it would take to become an Olympian. Four years later, not only did she qualify for the trials, but she also represented the US in the 1,500-meter race at the Atlanta Olympics. And over her career, she participated in more than 200 competitions around the world.

Each individual has a different set of sparks or motivators that give them the expectation that they can reach an elite level in their field. Some people grew up in an environment of high achievement because their parents or other people close to them had achieved exceptional success. Some have seen friends and peers shatter unbreakable boundaries. Some were placed in an environment filled with high performers and found out they could keep up.

The expectation of high achievement from yourself is also known as a culture of striving and is a trait not only demonstrated by the elite but also by the most elite of the elite—the highest-achieving exceptionals.

British researchers Lew Hardy, Matthew Barlow, Lynne Evans and their colleagues have performed ground-breaking research to understand the factors that create exceptional performance in sport. They studied elite athletes who were among the best in Britain, as well as super-elites, who were even more decorated, having won multiple medals (including at least one gold medal) at either the Olympics or their sport's world championships.[9] Their research presented an in-depth psychosocial assessment of the characteristics of the most accomplished athletes.

The researchers found that just about every exceptional individual came from an environment that promoted a culture of striving, which was a combination of four factors:

[9]Lew Hardy et al., 'Great British Medalists: Psychosocial Biographies of Super-Elite and Elite Athletes from Olympic Sports.' *Progress in Brain Research* 232 (2017): 1–119, Doi:10.1016/ bs.pbr.2017.03.004.

- An environment and expectation of achievement
- An environment with a strong work ethic
- An environment that is highly competitive
- An environment that places a high value on mastery and outcome

Let's take a more in-depth look at these four factors.

Many of the most exceptional individuals grew up in an environment where there was an expectation, not just a desire, of high achievement. To achieve excellence and try their very best was the norm. They shared a belief that exceptional performance was something that they could attain and that it was not something reserved only for people you see on TV.

Even though these athletes came from an environment of striving, their motivators to exceed were varied. Some aimed for high achievement because their parents had achieved exceptional success in a field, their siblings, friends or peers had gained prominence in a domain or because the environment they were in had many high performers.

Exceptionals also come from an environment where a strong work ethic has been instilled into them early in their journey. A common theme expressed by the most accomplished people is the phrase 'no one will outwork me'. People with extraordinary achievements have seen, from very early on, a positive link between effort and outcome. The culture they are in has led them to believe that if they work hard and consistently put in the effort, the results will be there, and consequently, they are not afraid to put in the effort.

Many exceptionals also grew up in a continually competitive environment where they had to earn every little success they achieved. From a young age, nothing was 'given' easily. They had to cross high bars to reap the rewards of accomplishing something. Being competitive from an early age, even in unrelated events, exposed the elites to the stress and pressure that was required for them to win later in life.

The most exceptional people were also exposed to an environment that placed value on both mastery (getting better at a task) and outcome (having positive results from doing it well). They wanted to get better to see how good they could get; the results they achieved were the by-product of attaining mastery. The competition was important and they wanted to do their best, but they did not focus solely on their results. They also focused on achieving their possible best. People with a focus only on outcome were less likely to become truly exceptional because their focus was primarily on results and not on improvement. Being exceptional is more than just keeping score.

Most exceptionals have emerged from an environment that has supported their drive to excellence. Sometimes, as in the case of the Polgár sisters, you may need to create that environment. Similar to the Polgár sisters, Venus and Serena Williams's unparalleled success on the tennis court was influenced by a shared environment that was created for them to excel: Their rise to the top started with their father, Richard, who drafted a detailed 78-page plan for his daughters' ascension to the top of the tennis world. The girls were not even five years old when he wrote down his process but it eventually shaped two of the most prolific champions in tennis history. Venus and Serena grew up in an environment created for tennis excellence, with the early expectation that they would be the best players in the game—a feat they both achieved.

SHAPING YOUR ENVIRONMENT

Being in a high-achievement environment plays a vital role in how you maximize your potential. It certainly is easier for us to influence the physical environment we require for success over the social environment. We can't go back in time and change our social setting to recreate the culture of striving we should have had in the past. But it is never too late. If you want to achieve excellence in anything, you should put yourself in an environment filled with like-minded people who pull you up and motivate you to excel. 'You are only as good as the company you keep' may be an adage, but it is true. Being surrounded by people who don't push you to excel or who bring you down is not going to help you achieve your aspirations. Life's too short to hang out with them.

There is no doubt that the environment you find yourself in shapes your performance and abilities. But sometimes you need to shape your environment into catalysing you to becoming extraordinary. If you find yourself not headed in the right direction, you may need to go back to the drawing board and rethink everything about who you are and what you truly want to become.

Your transformation starts with placing yourself in the physical, social and motivational settings that positively influence your performance. Sometimes you require a complete makeover, something that the All Blacks, the New Zealand national rugby team, needed.

Despite historically being a successful rugby team (winning 75 per cent of their international matches over the past 100 years), in 2004, the All Blacks team was in a slump, having suffered a few key losses. After a particularly hard loss against South Africa (another rugby powerhouse), the team was at a low point, with the players engaging in bouts of binge drinking and misbehaviour. The coaches viewed this as a wake-up call and needed to create a renewed motivational climate to have the team return to its former glory.

Creating a new and positive environment meant changing everything the team took for granted at the time. For example, the team switched from a system of autocratic management (where coaches made unilateral decisions) to a democratic and dual management system where players and coaches were both responsible for setting the team strategy. A new motto for the team was adopted: 'Better people make better All Blacks'. The new slogan was something that went straight to the heart of the characteristics the team wanted to instil in the players. Having players strive to become better in every way helped them achieve excellence in the field.

The entire environment was redesigned to improve motivation and excellence—and it worked. Players began to feel a greater responsibility for the team. Wearing the black jersey was given a special meaning and the players recognized this honour. A sense of pride was instilled in the organization. The team believed that excellence was expected, as that was the All Blacks legacy. The results of this environmental makeover soon began to manifest itself as performance on the field: The team won an astonishing 85 per cent of their international matches from 2004 to 2011.[10]

It is not too late for you to create an environment that drives you to perform your best. You may need to revisit the most fundamental questions about what you want to achieve and what you want your legacy to be. Then place yourself in a position that allows you to do your best work. Surround yourself with the people, the ideas, the resources and the mindset that brings out the very best in you. Only when you are in the environment that promotes sustained excellence will you be able to achieve it.

---

[10]Ken Hodge, Graham Henry, and Wayne Smith, 'A Case Study of Excellence in Elite Sport: Motivational Climate in a World Championship Team.' *The Sport Psychologist* 28 (2014): 60–74.

4

BELIEVE YOU CAN DO IT

During the summer of 1991, on a sweltering triple-digit day in Arizona, 40 wide-eyed young men were crammed into a tight conference room at a cheap motel just outside Phoenix for their first meeting. As uncomfortable as the surroundings were, the group could not have been more excited. They had just won the athletic lottery: The Milwaukee Brewers, a major league baseball team, had just drafted them. They were now professional baseball players. Their lifelong dream had finally come true.

It didn't matter that they still had five levels of minor league play to go through before they saw the shining lights of the major league. It didn't matter that most of them would never see those lights. It didn't matter that most of their contracts were for nothing, maybe a few thousand dollars—indeed, not enough for any kind of financial security. Nothing mattered except the hope and the possibilities. The future was as bright as the Arizona sun they played in every day.

The meeting was led by a gruff, 56-year-old former pitcher who was responsible for shaping the newly drafted rookies. A lifer in the sport, he was quick to point out the brutal realities of major league baseball. He told the young recruits that in a good draft year, 'maybe two of you will make it to the majors. And that's just getting there. It's easy to get there; it's harder to stay.'

A young Jeff Cirillo remembers taking a long look around the room, at all the other hopefuls, every single one of them filled with talent, energy and potential, and thinking to himself, 'I wonder who the other guy is.'

There was no wavering. There was no doubt. Cirillo just knew deep inside that if two people made it to the big time, he would be one of them. If only one made it, it would be him. He wasn't being brash or cocky; he simply had the inner belief that he would be successful. Yes, it would take a lot physically, mentally and emotionally to get there. But there was no doubt in his mind that he was up to the task.

And he did make it. He had a successful 14-year career in the major leagues, with a lifetime batting average of nearly .300, a pretty remarkable achievement.

But he wasn't supposed to make it. Cirillo was an eleventh-round pick who signed an $8,000 contract. During that draft year, about 300 players were picked ahead of him, pretty demoralizing for a star from the University of Southern California.

The top picks were signing contracts worth a few

hundred thousand dollars just to play in the minor leagues. One of the numerous unwritten rules in baseball is a common sense one: Protect your investment. When a team pays $500,000 to sign a prospect, they do everything they can to nurture and bring out the talent. This prospect is offered every opportunity to succeed, if only because the team has made a big bet on his potential. The team looks brilliant when the player does well, and they look pretty inept if their vaunted rookie turns out to be a dud.

The $8,000 contract meant that the organization didn't have a lot of faith in Cirillo, so they made a meagre investment in his prospects. Yes, he had been drafted, but getting to the cathedral of the majors was so out of the realm of possibility that no one expected him to make it. Since there wasn't a substantial investment in Cirillo, there would be no downside to the team if he didn't perform well.

Imagine yourself in his situation: Any one of a multitude of reasons could mean an early end to your dreams. Maybe the coach wouldn't like you, perhaps you'd get injured, you'd just not play well on certain days, somebody else would be just a little more impressive or there would be little need for players in your position to advance. As an eleventh-round pick, you'd get cut without a second thought and no one would miss you.

As a result, every low-round draft pick has to navigate through many landmines just to be noticed, let alone advance to the next stage. The only way to survive is to have a deep belief within yourself that you will prevail, just as Cirillo did when he looked around the room to size up his fellow rookies and try to guess who else, besides him, would break through and play in the major leagues.

At some point, we have all experienced this inner confidence, the calm feeling where we know we can succeed at a task before we even start it. The belief that this time, we are just going to nail it. When we experience that feeling, we perform at a higher level. We have set ourselves up for success, and we deliver. It is not false optimism or hope. It is just the inner knowledge and faith that no matter the odds against us, we will be successful. That positive belief influences how we perform the task.

In psychology, this confidence in our own abilities is called *self-efficacy*. Introduced by psychologist Albert Bandura, self-efficacy is an individual's belief in their innate capability to achieve their goals. According to Bandura, it is not sufficient for individuals to possess the skills and knowledge to perform a task; they must also have the conviction that they can achieve it successfully.[11] In other words, someone with high self-efficacy has an unshakable belief in their ability to complete a particular task and, consequently, is more likely to be successful at it.

Belief in your abilities is often a more reliable predictor of success than your actual skills or capabilities. This means that your level of achievement at a task is influenced more by whether you believe you can achieve it than whether

[11]Anthony R. Artino Jr., 'Academic Self-Efficacy: From Educational Theory to Instructional Practice.' *Perspectives on Medical Education* 1,2 (2012): 76–85, doi:10.1007/s40037-012-0012-5.

you have developed the skills and capabilities to achieve it. Such is the power of the mind. Cirillo believed he would make it to the major leagues even though he did not yet possess the skill set. This is a trait that is shared by all exceptionals.

The higher your self-efficacy—the belief you have about your capabilities—the more effort and persistence you are likely to put into a task, and, consequently, the more success you are likely to achieve. And while having self-efficacy does not equate to having the skills required to attaining your goals, the two factors are related.

Belief and skills are linked by reciprocal causation, which means that the functioning of one component depends on the functioning of the other. In other words, the more skilled you are at something, the higher your belief that you will succeed, and the more you believe that you will succeed, the more your skill set will stretch to meet the belief.

When you have the confidence and belief that you will overcome all barriers in your path, you will open yourself and allow all the other elements of excellence, such as effort, persistence and commitment, to flow through you and help you achieve your goals. If you doubt yourself, you have failed before you start because you are inhibiting yourself and will not put in the necessary effort to succeed. With the right degree of self-efficacy, you start off expecting to be successful in an endeavour, and if you don't achieve that success, you are surprised.

The results you can have with a positive belief in yourself are tremendous. A vast body of research conducted around the world over the past few decades has shown that having high self-efficacy has a positive effect on performance. One of the earliest landmark studies on self-efficacy involved researchers assigning participants in an experiment randomly to one of two groups.[12] The two groups were similar in every respect, except that one was labelled as a high self-efficacy group, and the other was categorized as a low self-efficacy group. Both groups then participated in leg-strength exercises against opponents to determine who had the most leg strength.

The researchers told the first group that their opponents were injured and had strained ligaments, leading the participants to believe they were likely to win. The researchers told the second group that their opponents were varsity athletes, effectively encouraging the participants to believe they would lose. Additionally, the researchers informed the first group that their opponents had performed poorly on their leg strength exercises and mentioned to the second group that their opponents had done well on them.

In taking these steps, the researchers artificially manipulated the self-efficacy of each group. They increased the self-efficacy of one group by making them believe they were stronger than their opponents and were very likely to win and they decreased the self-efficacy of the second group by making them believe they were weaker than their opponents.

---

[12]Haley Barrows, 'Why We Need to Practice Self-Efficacy.' *Medium*, 5 January 2018, https:// medium.com/performance-science/why-we-need-to-practice-self-efficacy-decb90a04e4, Accessed on 1 August 2020.

All the participants then performed the same exercises, with leg strength being measured for each participant. As you might guess, the results were staggering. The high self-efficacy group performed considerably better than the low self-efficacy group. The actual difference between the two groups was not in the power of their legs, but rather, in what they believed—their self-efficacy.

The power of self-efficacy is enormous. It lets people with lesser capacity outperform people with higher capacity. If you don't believe you can achieve something or you don't think you have the skills to pull off an activity, you will likely end up failing at it. The famous quote, attributed to Henry Ford, 'Whether you think you can or whether you think you can't, you're right,' summarizes this sentiment well.

Many exceptionals believed very early on that they would become the best in the world in their fields. It was this self-efficacy that kept them going through the rigors and pain of attaining their long-term goal. People with higher self-efficacy are willing to work harder, endure more sacrifices and invest more of their time and effort because they believe they will be the best. Those who don't believe in themselves will not commit to putting in the effort that is required to become the best.

INCREASING YOUR SELF-EFFICACY

There is no question that self-efficacy is necessary to achieve distinction in your field. We know this not because of all the research conducted in the space, but because we have all experienced that feeling. Sometimes, we just have confidence and know beforehand that we are going to be successful at an endeavour and, at those times, we usually are. That is the feeling we want to experience more often as we go down our journey toward becoming exceptional. The question, therefore, is, '*How do we build that feeling?*' The good news is that self-efficacy is not a static capability. It is something that can be grown and developed.

Don't misunderstand: You don't have to be the brash and overconfident type of person who believes they are good at everything; these are the people who often lack belief in themselves. Instead, you need the quiet inner confidence in your ability to perform a specific task at a certain level.

We call people who have this confidence *clutch performers*. If everything were on the line, you would want Michael Jordan to take the final shot on the basketball court or Tiger Woods to make the all-important putt. You want them not because they have the best stats for shooting or putting (maybe they do, but quite likely, they don't), you want them because they know how to come through when they need to. That is something that comes from believing in your ability and knowing that your best work will appear when you need it most.

To understand and improve self-efficacy, let's first distinguish it from other types of self-worth. Specifically, self-efficacy is the belief that you can achieve a specific goal. This is important because it is the specificity that drives performance. It is different from other measures of self-worth, like self-concept and self-esteem. Self-concept is a general belief in your skills in a given domain and self-esteem is your belief about yourself at a higher level of abstraction and is related to how you value or like yourself.

Self-efficacy is exemplified by specific statements, such as 'I can run tomorrow's 10K race in 35 minutes,' as opposed to a more general self-concept statement like 'I am a good runner'. Or 'I can successfully offer a 10 per cent discount and close the deal at my meeting today' instead of 'I am good at sales.' Or 'I can lose 10 pounds in six months' compared to 'I can stay healthy.' Or 'I can write the code for this feature to work' versus 'I am a good software developer.' Specificity is the key.

Experiencing Success and Achieving Mastery

The best way to improve self-efficacy is by experiencing success. Psychologists refer to this as *mastery*. When you do well at something, your belief and your confidence in your abilities grow. Remember the skills that you determined were your natural talents? When you use those skills to achieve something—to reach a goal—your self-efficacy grows with each success.

You can also increase your self-efficacy by being successful at increasingly challenging tasks, which leads you to continuously get better. You can reach a state of perpetual improvement by setting and achieving goals that are slightly beyond your reach or that slightly exceed your actual capabilities. This modest overestimation, setting targets just beyond your ability, will get you to stretch and apply the effort and persistence required to attain them. As you achieve these stretch targets, you get more comfortable in believing in yourself and pushing for more.

Set a goal that is slightly beyond what you can accomplish today and make a point to achieve it. Just this simple act of achieving a goal beyond your current capacity will increase your belief in yourself. This will lead to setting the next goal that is slightly higher, and the next. As you succeed, you learn that you are better than you thought you were; if you fail, you know where to improve.

Don't just set modest goals; set lofty ones, as all exceptionals do. But convert them to specific and immediate objectives. Let each milestone you achieve become a stepping-stone toward your more substantial and ambitious goals. As you continue to do this, the cumulative power of what you believe and what you can achieve becomes immeasurable. Excellence is nothing but a series of continual improvements that add up to extraordinary outcomes.

While mastering a task improves self-efficacy, the opposite is also possible. Setting unattainable goals may set you up for failure, which may reduce your self-efficacy. But the good news is that once you have a high degree of belief in yourself, failures don't hurt as much. You will begin to attribute failures that you inevitably experience along the way to factors like being unprepared, not your inability. With greater ability in your talent comes a more realistic understanding of your skills, which allows you to pinpoint the areas in which you need improvement.

Vicarious experiences

While task mastery is the best way to improve self-efficacy, you can also improve it through vicarious experiences. Seeing others achieve success can serve as a big motivator, especially if they are people you consider peers or people with abilities similar to yours. As discussed in the previous chapter, runner Juli Benson's motivational visit to the Olympic trials, where she saw people she knew participating and succeeding—and knew she could do it too—is a prime example of how a vicarious experience can monumentally increase one's self-efficacy.

A vast body of research indicates that observing others can serve as an impetus for improving self-efficacy. When you watch someone you consider a peer accomplish something impressive, your belief that you can do the same increases. The general statement that illustrates the vicarious effect of self-efficacy is, 'If they can do it, so can I.' Conversely, observing an individual with similar abilities fail at a task can weaken your self-efficacy.

Watching role models (say, athletes on TV) or others who are already exceptional can sometimes serve as a vicarious stimulus to self-efficacy. But it is less impactful than seeing a peer do something extraordinary. Overall, though, if you want to do better, witnessing people excel will give you more confidence in your abilities.

Verbal Persuasion

Verbal persuasion, or feedback and instruction, is another tool you can use to improve your self-efficacy. Verbal persuasion is a weaker driver of self-efficacy than task mastery or vicarious experiences, but it is still influential. You can be persuaded by parents, role models, mentors, coaches or co-workers, all of whom have the power to persuade you to strive for achievements you believe are beyond your capability. People may see something in you that you don't and may be able to motivate you effectively. Exceptionals in every field can point to people they admire who gave them that boost of confidence by seeing something in them that they didn't yet see in themselves.

For that communication to be most useful, it needs to be positive and specific. Thus, a generalized statement such as 'you can do this' is, at best, marginally useful. Instead, comments with precise instruction, pointed feedback or specific expectations about your performance or abilities are more helpful than vague encouragements. Verbal persuasion works best if the person who influences you is someone you trust or has credibility in your domain. Find a coach or mentor and ask them to honestly evaluate your skills.

THE FIRST STEP TO ACHIEVING EXCELLENCE

Belief in yourself and the confidence that you can achieve something magnificent is the start of your journey to becoming exceptional. The mission to the top is simply too hard to complete without an ongoing optimism in your abilities. It is only the confidence you have about your success that will let you put in the work and effort to be successful. The belief you have in your capabilities will allow you to stretch and achieve bigger and bigger goals. Your self-efficacy is a form of constructive thinking that will allow you to better cope with the hardships you will endure, continually make improvements and reach for higher and higher goals.

The most exceptional people show an enormous amount of self-efficacy in their abilities. They view the challenges they face as things they can overcome and not as things that will diminish them. Their belief in themselves allows them to stay committed to their goals for years and even decades. They believe failure is simply due to a lack of skills that they can develop, not a reason to give up on their dreams. They express a high degree of commitment to their goals and, as a result, don't give up.

As you commence your journey toward being exceptional, check in with yourself to ensure that you genuinely believe you will be successful. To help you get there, start focusing on the smaller goals along the way because it is these small successes that increase your self-efficacy.

Do it the Michael Jordan way. Jordan, considered by many as the greatest basketball player of all time, achieved his amazing feats by focusing on smaller goals. To lead the National Basketball Association (NBA) in scoring, which he did just about every year, he needed to average 32 points a game for an entire season. While that might sound like a lot, when broken into specific smaller goals, that was only eight points a quarter, a bite-size target of scoring four times over 12 minutes. Jordan knew he could do that, and the more he did it, the more he was able to believe he could do better. After having done it for three quarters, his belief about success in the fourth quarter would be that much stronger. And as his record shows, there is likely no better fourth-quarter player than Jordan.

When you consistently set and achieve your targets, you build the confidence that you can do so much more, and your belief in yourself continues to grow. It is this self-belief that takes you to the very top of your pyramid.

5

THE MYTH OF THE SOLO SUPERSTAR

I n 2015, scientists from CERN, a particle physics lab near Geneva, Switzerland, published their research quantifying the most precise estimate of the mass of the Higgs boson, a subatomic particle considered foundational to the understanding of the universe. Perhaps just as significant as the findings was the fact that the paper had more than 5,000 authors.

Twenty-four of the 33 pages of the article were devoted to listing the authors' names and their institutions.[13]

The research on the Higgs boson, the particle that gives

---

[13]Davide Castelvecchi, 'Physics Paper Sets Record with More Than 5,000 Authors.' *Nature*, 15 May 2015, https://www.nature.com/news/physics-paper-sets-record-with-more-than-5-000-authors-1.17567#:~:text=Physics%20paper%20sets%20record%20with%20more%20than%205%2C000%20authors,size%20of%20the%20Higgs%20boson. Accessed on 1 August 2020.

all matter its mass, is a critical breakthrough in physics and in human understanding of the universe. The 5,000 experts who collaborated on this research remind us that we have come a long way in uncovering excellence from the era when scientists toiled alone in dusky labs to create world-shaping discoveries.

Although the idea of a solo superstar is romantic, it's not how things work in any field. The image of a lone scientist, like Isaac Newton and Albert Einstein, is a figure of the past, and even for those historical exceptionals, it is rarely an accurate picture. Doing exceptional work no longer is a solo affair—if it ever was. It requires a team and sometimes a small army of people working together. The creation of new knowledge is an increasingly complex undertaking that virtually no one can manage individually. Over the past century, the average number of authors per scientific paper has increased from one to more than five today. Scientists used to work alone, then in pairs, then in teams and today, in massively networked communities. The Higgs boson paper is not alone in having a large group of collaborators; the article on the initial sequencing and analysis of the human genome, published in *Nature*, has over 2,000 authors.[14] For further evidence of what it takes to become exceptional in science, look no further than the gradual aging of Nobel laureates. Today, the average age of a Nobel laureate in physics is between 60 and 70 years, compared to the

---

[14]'Initial Sequencing and Analysis of the Human Genome.' *Nature News*, www.nature.com/articles/35057062#author-information. Accessed on 1 August 2020.

mid-forties during the first half of the twentieth century. In all of the science-based Nobel awards, recipients have been steadily aging over time. Even the beginning of the journey into scientific research is getting longer, with the average age at which people obtain their PhDs steadily increasing. Science is growing more complicated as there is far more information required to create new knowledge than ever before, which is why it is harder to excel at it individually. Large-scale and impactful scientific research requires information crossover from different disciplines and a host of abilities that weren't necessary a few decades ago.

Ground-breaking research doesn't merely need exceptional scientists and researchers; it also needs people with programming skills, data access skills, statistical expertise and with project management skills to name a few. While the Nobel Prize goes to the lead researcher or two, the breakthroughs they created would simply not be possible without the amalgamation of knowledge and resources from a highly efficient cohort.

While the need for collaboration is readily apparent in creating excellence in science, the same is true for every discipline. The most exceptional individuals never achieve brilliance by themselves. Sure, they are immensely talented, but the outsized success of extraordinary individuals in every field—be it Serena Williams, Usain Bolt, Steve Jobs or Bill Gates—is based on a team of expert collaborators. Excellence today is multidisciplinary and a solo approach simply does not work, primarily because it keeps getting harder and harder to achieve greatness.

There is an exponentially increasing amount of insight and sophistication required to become outstanding and as the world gets more complex, the solo superstar becomes more of a relic. To become exceptional in your field, whatever it may be, you need to learn to embrace complexity and to thrive in an increasingly networked and cooperative world.

INCREASING COMPLEXITY IS A UNIVERSAL RULE

Researchers from England's University of Bath studying fossils from the last 550 million years found that all organisms developed in only one direction: from simple to complex.[15] They observed that evolution always results in a form with more complex structures and features than before. The move toward increasing complexity is about as close to a universal rule of evolution as possible.

In a way, this makes perfect sense. We have evolved from single-cell microbes to teeming cities and vast ecosystems. We share the planet with almost nine million other species and each one has increased in complexity over time. The ones unable to handle the increased complexity demanded by the world have become extinct.

Increasing complexity is not limited to life forms. Complexity increases in your work, relationships, business,

---

[15]'First "Rule" Of Evolution Suggests That Life Is Destined to Become More Complex.' *ScienceDaily*, 18 March 2008, www.sciencedaily.com/releases/2008/03/080317171027.htm. Accessed on 1 August 2020.

sport and in just about every other area of life. The bar to be exceptional is raised higher with each passing generation. Jesse Owens's gold medal time of 10.3 seconds in the 100-meter race at the 1936 Berlin Olympics would not even qualify him for any Olympic team in the world today. For further proof, simply look at the body of output of the greatest pianists or violin or cello players from 50 years ago. You will find dozens of videos on YouTube today of children under 10 playing the same instruments with a comparable level of skill.

As the bar continually gets higher, every area becomes more complex and harder to manage single-handedly. Anyone aiming for excellence needs to realize that achieving brilliance becomes less of an individual pursuit and requires increased coordination of different areas of expertise.

The World Economic Forum understands this. It has listed the ability to deal with complexity as the top skill required for employees to thrive in the coming years.[16] As society progresses, the amount of knowledge we have to deal with increases. As a result, you need to understand not only the vast number of advances directly in your field but also the even more significant set of advances in related and unrelated domains that will help your cause. Very often, it is new information from other fields that makes the difference between good and great.

---

[16]Alex Gray, 'The 10 Skills You Need to Thrive in the Fourth Industrial Revolution.' *World Economic Forum*, 19 January 2016, https://www.weforum.org/agenda/2016/01/the-10-skills-you-need-to-thrive-in-the-fourth-industrial-revolution. Accessed on 1 August 2020.

Before 2010, tennis ace Novak Djokovic was a very good player and competitive on the world stage but he was not one of the all-time greats of the game. Even though he trained harder than most tennis professionals and was fanatical about his fitness, he suffered from mid-match breakdowns, where he felt a loss of strength and energy that he found difficult to overcome. Often that was just enough to cost him the match.

During the quarterfinal match at the 2010 Australian Open, Djokovic had yet another one of his low-energy moments. During one of the breaks, he sat slumped in his chair, having trouble breathing and finding it hard to get back up and continue the match (which he eventually lost).[17]

It just so happened that a Serbian compatriot and nutritionist, Dr Igor Cetojevic, was flipping channels on his TV and stumbled upon the match. Although he was not much of a tennis fan, he immediately recognized why Djokovic was having his mini-meltdown. He surmised that this drain of energy resulted from food sensitivities.

Eventually, Cetojevic was able to meet Djokovic and discuss his theory with the tennis star. After running some tests, he confirmed his early diagnosis. Djokovic was indeed intolerant to wheat and dairy products and this affected his body when it was stressed to the max, as it would be in the middle to late stages of an intense tennis match.

[17]Paul Newman, 'Revealed: The Diet That Saved Novak Djokovic.' *The Independent*, 19 August 2016, https://www.independent.co.uk/sport/tennis/revealed-the-diet-that-saved-novak- djokovic-8775333.html. Accessed on 1 August 2020.

For someone who grew up in a family that owned a pizza restaurant, it would be a challenge to give up gluten, but Djokovic did just that. He switched to a gluten-free and plant-based diet at the nutritionist's suggestion and almost immediately felt better, had more energy and slept better.

But the longer-term effects of changing his diet were monumental. The very next year, he won 10 tournaments, including three of the four grand slam championships, achieved the number one ranking in the world for the first time and set a record for prize money earned in a single year ($12 million). It was one of the most dominant performances by any player in tennis during a season. His performance was so impressive that former world number one Pete Sampras called it the best tennis season he had ever seen in his lifetime. Rafael Nadal, himself an all-time tennis great and a fierce rival to Djokovic, called it the highest level of tennis he had ever seen.

Djokovic was always an elite tennis player, but it was the knowledge he gained from another discipline (nutrition science) and from another expert that made him exceptional. Tennis is about as much of an individual sport as you can find. Still, the best players have achieved their success as a result of assimilating distributed knowledge and teamwork. Today, Djokovic's team of experts includes coaches, a yoga instructor, a fitness trainer, a manager, a physiotherapist, a hitting partner and a racket technician, among others. His team of coaches and trainers travel with him 11 months of the year. Each member of the group is a specialist who provides the guidance that helps Djokovic manage the vast and multiple knowledge streams required for becoming elite.

The most successful people—those who create exceptional outcomes and achieve their possible best—are the ones who have learned to embrace an increasingly multifaceted world and use it to their advantage. Complexity will never travel in the other direction, toward simplicity. While we may dream of a simpler time, it is not going to happen and will not lead us to the path of excellence. Exceptional output from solo efforts will continue to decrease and extraordinary returns will invariably go to the most high-functioning teams.

Very often, the advice we get is that the best way to manage complexity is through simplifying things. While convenient and comfortable, this thought may not always be helpful. You don't achieve excellence by attempting to make a complicated problem simple. You achieve excellence by embracing its complexity and relying on expert knowledge to help you create simple and elegant solutions that capture and address all of the intricacies inherent in a complex problem.

DISTRIBUTED EXPERTISE

Elite athletes need to know more about training methods, nutrition, physics, physiology, biomechanics, psychology, contract negotiation and a host of other topics than they ever did before. You need to do the same in your profession. Make a list of the parallel domains that you believe can influence your field. Or better yet, ask someone who has reached the pinnacle in your field to list the areas they have had to learn and the expertise they have needed to lean on. As you go through this list, evaluate whether you have the necessary expertise and support so you can draw the knowledge from these areas. You have to learn to be able to shoulder the increasing volume of information to reach the top.

Even if you are a brilliant polymath, it will be virtually impossible for you to become an expert in every discipline. Consequently, you can only be effective by distributing expertise and learning from the knowledge of others. We know modern athletes like Serena Williams and Novak Djokovic have an entourage of experienced professionals helping them in each area, and they can only become exceptional if this team works in unison toward a common goal. You will find people at the top of every profession supported by experts. And while it is easy to hire an entourage after achieving success, every exceptional can point to the people they learned from and leaned on during their formative years and credits others for lending that expertise and knowledge.

Sir Isaac Newton, one of the world's most exceptional scientists, attributed his world-changing accomplishments to the knowledge he gained from others. His timeless quote, 'If I have seen further, it is by standing on the shoulders of giants,' highlights the need for distributed expertise and adopting the learning of other experts, even at a time when the world was so much simpler. Newton leaned on the in-depth knowledge from authorities in fields as diverse as chemistry, mathematics, optics, religion, history and philosophy to create his exceptional theories that have left an indelible mark on the world.

Don't confuse distributed learning with teamwork, as we colloquially know it. While collaboration is essential, distributed learning implies that exceptional output is never the result of knowledge in a single discipline. You must continuously scan areas outside of your domain and bring in relevant information to advance your work. The people who do this the best are the ones who achieve the most.

New thoughts and ideas may not appear serendipitously for you as they did for Djokovic. You gain knowledge by having an open mind and a thirst for learning, so you need to seek out new ways of thinking, often without knowing how they could affect your efforts. You need to consume as much information as you can and trust that exposure to other fields will open your mind in unimaginable ways. Knowledge truly is power.

Peter Diamond, the distinguished 2010 Nobel laureate in Economics, is an example of someone who sought knowledge from a new discipline without knowing directly how it would apply to his field. Diamond, a long-time student and scholar of economics, credits much of the ground-breaking work that led to his Nobel Prize to the classes he took at Harvard Law School, even though he wasn't a student there.

Diamond started his career as an economist with a bang, having performed innovative research that resulted in the publication of landmark theories early in his career.

But after those successes, he found he wasn't growing professionally and needed something new to stimulate his thinking. Diamond wanted to expose himself to a different set of questions, grounded in a different discipline. He believed this was necessary to help him conduct impactful research. As a result, he decided to attend classes in law.

He signed up for a yearlong class and applied himself to learning a brand-new discipline. In doing so, his mind was exposed to new ideas, thereby giving him a new way of thinking. He took this learning opportunity very seriously, attending law classes for four years and even sitting in on exams with other law students. Ultimately, it was this crossover between law and economics that led to his breakthrough work on demand and supply of labour that eventually culminated in the Nobel Prize.

Diamond is not alone; exceptionals in every field have an open mind. They are voracious consumers of new knowledge and information, not just in their discipline, but in a variety of areas. The thirst for learning opens their minds to new ideas, some of which they apply to become better at their field. They realize that focusing solely on a narrow area is limiting because when you have no further knowledge or no new ideas, you have no new ways of improving.

Cross-pollination of ideas plays a significant role in the accomplishments of the exceptionals. Of course, you need to specialize in your primary subject to become competent and accomplished, but to become the best, you need to push the boundaries of your field. The best way to do that is to learn from other fields and from what has worked in other areas. Every domain in the world is growing steadily, which means there is so much more knowledge available for you to use. The people who take advantage of this growth opportunity will have the most success.

The easiest way to learn from other disciplines is through reading—about anything and everything. Just about every exceptional is an avid reader and consumer of information. They realize they don't know everything and need to have their minds open to learning new things. You never know when something you read or learn can help you with a problem you are trying to solve.

Find a field that is not your primary talent, preferably something you know little about. Read a book on the subject and see what new ideas emerge that you might apply to your specialty.

BUILD YOUR IMPROVEMENT COMMUNITY

Of course, it is easy to hire an entourage of experts tasked with making you better when you are at the peak of your profession. A top 10 tennis player, earning tens of millions of dollars a year in prize money and endorsements, can afford to hire a nutritionist, a physical therapist, a manager, a psychologist, a personal trainer, a statistician and a team of traveling coaches. But even if you haven't yet reached the pinnacle and don't have millions to spend, you can still bring in the power of distributed expertise by creating your own improvement community, a group of people that you trust will help you and motivate you to get better.

The people in your improvement community may be coaches, co-workers, managers, spouses, parents, people you look up to, experts in specific areas or anyone else you believe can help you get better. The only requirement is that these people are fully vested in your success and tell you the truth.

Picture your improvement community as a wheel. You are at the centre or the hub of your community. The other members are the spokes and the outward-facing participants who contribute their own experience, expertise and knowledge. You are then responsible for integrating the information your community brings to you and applying it in the ways that best serve you.

Your improvement community does not solely have to consist of people that you know. It could be a virtual community made up of people whose work you read and learn from, people you follow or those who share their experiences and motivate or inspire you. Your improvement community provides you with the tools and knowledge that make you perform at a higher level.

BE INFLUENCED

Glen Mills served as more than just a coach for Usain Bolt. He was a mentor and a powerful influence in Bolt's life. Mills was as invested in Bolt achieving his possible best as Bolt himself was. Mills had all of the skills to be the perfect influence on Bolt's progression. He cared, was knowledgeable about the domain and knew what it would take to succeed, not only technically but also emotionally. He was able to create an environment that fostered Bolt's talents and efforts to result in unmatched success.

Every exceptional can point to their version of Coach Mills—someone who has mentored, guided or influenced them through their early stages and helped them gain the confidence that they could accomplish anything. These influencers or mentors could be coaches, parents, teachers, competitors, colleagues, business partners, senior leaders, spouses or other positive role models who bring out the best by providing technical skills, emotional support and confidence.

Mentors play an essential role in the development of talent because they provide a nurturing environment that allows the exceptionals to believe in themselves and consequently feel motivated to do their best work. Even years or decades later, when exceptionals reflect on their career and what made them who they are, they can recall with great detail their relationship with their early mentors and the influence they had.

Jacob Nissly, the exceptional principal percussionist at the renowned San Francisco Symphony, has learnt his craft from many of the finest music instructors in the world. Still, he credits a little-known drum teacher from Iowa as his most significant influence. It was this tutor who exposed him to a new form of music (gospel), a new way of thinking about music, and skills that he never thought he would need. This instructor became a trusted mentor who gave him the confidence and taught him the discipline required to learn and become the best, which has served him well over his distinguished career.

Your own influence can come from anybody you look up to and who pushes you to be your best. John Lennon and Paul McCartney, the most celebrated song writing duo in history, deeply—perhaps unknowingly— influenced each other. While each was immensely talented, neither would have been as successful alone as they were together. They provided each other with mentoring, coaching, support, competition and encouragement. They helped each other write songs and often wrote songs together. They filled in musical voids that the other left open. They influenced each other through rivalry as well. The motivation and desire to outwrite each other elevated them to a level of excellence the musical world has not seen since. This cross-influence allowed them to keep getting better all the time.

FIND YOUR VILLAGE

It takes a village to become exceptional. It is not possible to make the trek to the top of the mountain alone. You will need the support of a mentor and a team of experts to guide and help you navigate the complicated journey. Even if you think you can do it alone, you most likely can't. The best in the world appear to stand alone, but they don't. They have the support of a set of people whom they trust and who provide necessary expert knowledge. They have built their community and their village, even if sometimes it needs to be a virtual one.

Every exceptional can point to the people who have influenced them, guided them and given them the confidence, tools and knowledge to succeed. Do you have a mentor who serves as a pillar and supports you and is as vested in your success as you are? If not, find someone you can open up to and who will encourage you. The world is complex and is becoming more so, and without the power of an improvement community you can rely on, the hard road to greatness will be a lot harder.

6

MICROEXCELLENCE

The 2008 Beijing Olympics made American swimmer Michael Phelps a household name. Phelps became the most prolific Olympic medallist, winning eight gold medals in Beijing. This feat is unmatched in the history of the Olympic Games—not just in the pool, but in any sport. It is an achievement as close to impossible as possible.

Of his eight victories, his seventh, the 100-meter butterfly event, was his most implausible. Going up against a strong field, the notoriously slow-starting Phelps was seventh out of eight swimmers at the halfway mark as he made a perfect turn on the far end wall. He had a lot of ground to make up, and being the elite performer that he is, he did just that during the final 50 meters. As he approached the finish, the race was tight; and with only a few meters to go, Phelps was barely a hair behind Milorad Čavić, the celebrated Serbian swimmer.

As Phelps closed in on the finish, he could either glide to reach the wall with his legs powering him on, which was the traditional way to close out a race, or he could take another stroke with his arms to propel him forward. But there wasn't enough room to take another stroke. He was coming up on the finishing wall, so the best he could do was take a half stroke.

Phelps decided to take the half stroke, whereas Čavić glided in. Since Phelps was lunging into the finish, he hit the timing pad with full force—and the power of that forceful impact gave Phelps the smallest margin of victory possible in a swimming race. Only 1/100th of a second separated Phelps and Čavić. They reached the wall at just about the same time, but the force that Phelps hit the pad with made the difference.

Phelps and his long-time coach Bob Bowman were both masters of detail. They had practiced this finish for years. While every swimmer in any Olympic final is a gifted athlete who works incredibly hard, one of the reasons Phelps wins consistently is because of his attention to the minutest of details. The technique to touch the wall is one that he and his coach had practiced repeatedly, and it proved to be quite likely the most crucial detail in Olympic history. Without it, he would not have won eight gold medals or set a new record that could last decades, if not lifetimes.

The 2008 finish was not an anomaly. Phelps displayed the same *microexcellence* in 2016, this time as a 31-year-old veteran during his final Olympic Games in Rio. At his signature event, the 200-meter fly, once again, it was his uncanny ability to hit the timing pad with force and efficiency that separated him by just 4/100ths of a second from the surging Japanese swimmer Masato Sakai.[18]

Phelps's attention to minutia that could impact his race is well documented. Other swimmers are in awe of his amazing attention to detail. Everything he does during and around major races is planned, and nothing is left to chance. He plans not just the specifics of what he will do in the pool at just about every meter of the race, but also everything he does outside of the water. This focus on the minutest of things removes any unknown or any variable that can impact performance. He even won a gold medal when he was 'blind' in the pool due to water clogging his goggles during an Olympic race. He swam the entire race without being able to see anything. He was able to do so by counting his strokes, so he knew exactly when he needed to flip at the wall and when to glide in for the finish.

Every exceptional, not just Phelps, has achieved distinction through a maniacal focus on detail; they have achieved excellence through microexcellence. The more they have broken down and worked on the minuscule elements of their domain, the higher they have been able to rise. They have been able to climb higher by diving lower and deeper into every detail and every microaction.

---

[18]Mary Beth Faller, 'Bob Bowman Uses Michael Phelps to Explain How to Achieve Excellence.' *Arizona State University*, 30 January 2017, https://universitycollege.asu.edu/ bob-bowman-uses-michael-phelps-explain-how-achieve-excellence. Accessed on 1 August 2020.

MICROEXCELLENCE

The most outstanding individuals, from all walks of life, have attained their greatness by focusing on the small, seemingly insignificant things, not just by focusing on the big stuff. The cumulative effect of small changes leads to significant outcomes. The exceptionals understand this, and while they set out with big goals, they improve with the use of systematic and surgical precision. Most of us also set big goals, but we try to tackle them all at once and want immediate results, and invariably, we fail. This is why most people are unable to keep their New Year's resolutions and abandon them well before they enter the shortest month of the year.

This approach of improving individual components and the minute and detailed aspects of an activity is called microexcellence. It means achieving excellence by focusing on the tiny little things that are under your control and are improvable. Very often, this attention to detail is ignored. Every outstanding individual has focused on these minor, seemingly unimportant things, but these multiple seemingly insignificant changes add up to substantial transformations and big gains over time. It is a lot easier to focus on manageable improvements where you see specific results than to chase big ideas that may lead nowhere. This dedicated focus on improvement in the smallest of tasks that no one wants to spend time on separates the elite few from others who are often more gifted and talented but never realize their full potential.

For example, Neil Peart, the virtuoso drummer of the Canadian progressive rock band Rush, was arguably one of the most respected musicians in modern music. After 25 years of exceptional performance for which he was already considered the world's greatest drummer, he decided to start taking lessons. His goal was to improve the minutia, the tiny details of his technique, so that his skills could continue to grow.

Peart sought out Freddie Gruber, a renowned teacher and coach of jazz drumming. Using this expanded improvement community—and taking advantage of knowledge from an adjacent field—Peart reinvented his playing, even changing the way he held his drumsticks. This focus on the fundamentals, the details of every strike, allowed him to continue perfecting his talent.

Other musicians might balk at the idea of beginning lessons after nearly three decades of professional success. Many rock musicians would scoff at the idea of incorporating jazz or swing techniques into their genre—thinking perhaps that these adjacent fields had little to offer theirs. But that is what separates talented from exceptional.

The players who don't focus on the details might have some success, but they will never be the best of the best. Exceptional performers like Peart diligently work hard on improving every minute aspect of their craft. The ones who focus on microexcellence make their mark, play in stadiums packed with adoring fans and earn tens of millions of dollars. Those who don't focus on the details are left with fading memories of glory from their garage band days.

EVERY DETAIL COUNTS

Sir Dave Brailsford, leader of Team Sky (now Team INEOS) and former performance director of British Cycling, revolutionized the sport with the introduction of the theory of marginal gains.

He believed that if you make a 1 per cent improvement in a host of areas, the cumulative benefits will be extraordinary. This theory of marginal gains, or what I refer to as microexcellence, has been credited for vaulting the British cycling team from being a mediocre performer to winning 16 gold medals over two Olympics and seven Tour de France wins in eight years.

The examples of microexcellence used by the British cycling team are legendary in the sports world.[19] Brailsford had the floors of the team truck painted pristine white to spot dust on the floor, because even the slightest amount of dust could potentially impair bike maintenance. This act alone wasn't enough to win a race or make any more than a borderline gain, but when added to a host of other small improvements, it made all the difference.

The Tour de France is a 21-day race of gruelling distances and climbs that saps every ounce of energy and strength from its riders. During the race, the cyclists sleep in 21 different hotels, each with different beds and pillows. When you ride six hours a day for three weeks straight, the

---

[19]'Viewpoint: Should We All Be Looking for Marginal Gains?' *BBC News*, 15 September 2015, https://www.bbc.com/news/magazine-34247629. Accessed on 1 August 2020.

slightest deprivation of rest can make a significant difference in performance. Brailsford had the team bus carry custom-designed mattresses and pillows for each rider, which were set up in each athlete's room so that the elements of rest and recovery were controlled and not left to chance. Again, this is a detail that in isolation is not going to win you the Tour de France, but in combination with all of the other minor changes, the results are staggering.

As this idea became a culture and a philosophy shared by all members of Brailsford's team, they kept searching for any and every area where they could make tiny improvements. Their goal was a marginal or 1 per cent gain in every aspect of their training and environment. Individually, each incremental change may have seemed unnecessary or random, but collectively, they helped create a powerhouse with a level of success that became the envy of the cycling world.

Becoming exceptional is never the result of focusing on a few 'important' areas; it is the cumulative effect of achieving excellence in countless small steps.

CONTINUOUS IMPROVEMENT

Excellence is a subjective concept. You know it when you see it and what may appear as excellent to one person may not be so for another. Even if you are at the ultimate pinnacle of your profession and have achieved a level of brilliance the world has never seen, and very few will ever match, you may not believe you have achieved excellence.

That is not necessarily a lack of self-belief; it may, in fact, be the ideal level of self-efficacy: Even though you might be the best, you can always get better. Your possible best is always just ahead.

In 2005, Roger Federer won 11 tennis titles, including two grand slams, and held the number one ranking for all 52 weeks of the year.[20] And within that, his performance on grass courts, where he had not lost a single match in three years, was especially spectacular.

His reaction to his grass-court play was, 'I definitely feel there's room for improvement.'

Excellence is based on the bar you set for yourself; that's why I refer to it as your *possible best*. No one can define excellence for you or determine whether you have achieved it. Most people are unable to fully use their abilities and consequently are unable to achieve the results they desire. However, your possible best is not an end goal. It's a shifting target, always just at the edge of your reach. To constantly seek your possible best, you need to improve every day.

Continuous improvement isn't about reaching lofty goals—at least not by jumping directly for them. Instead, build a ladder. Set manageable targets. Make small, incremental changes but make them constantly. Analyse your performance—not to self-criticize but to find areas for genuine improvement—and determine what works well and what needs fixing. These minor refinements of your

---

[20]Caroline Cheese, 'Roger Ready to Rewrite Records.' *BBC Sport*, 4 July 2005, http://news. bbc.co.uk/sport2/hi/tennis/4648467.stm. Accessed on 1 August 2020.

talent are the rungs of your ladder; you can then climb them one by one. Over time, they will add up to help you meet those lofty goals.

SUSTAINED EXCELLENCE

Achieving brilliance requires not just a great performance but continued, sustained excellence over time. This means that you need to be able to maintain your current levels of performance (without slippage), along with the ability to improve continually. The exceptionals focus on being excellent all the time instead of trying to peak at certain moments.

You can't become the best in your field if you only excel at certain moments. While people in some fields, like athletes or musicians, know well in advance precisely when they need to be at their peak (during their game, meet, match or concert), for most other professions, your peak performance will be required when you least expect it. You may be pulled into a critical meeting when you least expect, you may have to deliver a client presentation, design a product or perform a complicated surgery when it's needed, not when you have spent days preparing for it. Peak performance should not be reserved for a specific event; if you continually improve, you should always be at your peak.

Everyone wants to be excellent when it matters most, but the only way to be excellent when it matters most is to be excellent when it matters least. The best in the world do this by differentiating between their craft (the skills they learn) and their art (how they perform using those skills). They relentlessly work on getting better at their craft until it becomes ingrained into their minds and bodies. Then, when they need to be at their peak, they forget about the craft—the mechanics—and perform with mindless ease so that the art flows effortlessly through them.

The Performance Multiplier

Peak performance is a multiple of your sustained level of excellence. It happens when you prepare extensively for an event to ensure that all conditions are just right for your finest output to emerge. But the best way to enhance your peak performance is by raising your steady or everyday level of performance. If you elevate the bar for your daily level of performance, then your peak performances are going to be at an exponentially higher level.

Using simple math, let's assume that the level of competency in an event, say swimming, ranges from 0 to 10. At level 0, you don't know how to swim, and at level 10, you are an elite swimmer. Let's assume that when you prepare for a critical swim meet, you do everything you can to push yourself to your peak and you do 20 per cent better than you do at your sustained level.

Using this example, if your skill level is at 5, then at your peak, your performance, and perhaps your personal best, is at a level of 5 times 1.2, which is 6. If you set out to improve your base level by two points, from 5 to 7, your peak performance now rises to 7 times 1.2, which is 8.4—resulting in a 2.4-point increase in your peak performance. If you continue to keep improving your base, your peaks will keep getting higher.

Conversely, if you focus on improving your peak time by two points, or in other words, set a target for a new personal best of 8, you would need to push yourself hard to achieve that peak performance level. Instead, as shown above, by focusing on improving your base skills by the same amount, your peak performance would be substantially higher (8.4 versus 8) without explicitly trying to peak for a single performance.

A focus on sustaining and improving your ongoing level of ability is going to yield disproportionately higher dividends than a focus on preparing for one specific event after another, something most of us tend to do. In other words, a focus on your possible best—your sustained level of excellence—will help you more than a focus on your personal best based on peak performance.

ACHIEVING MICROEXCELLENCE

You can inculcate the concept of microexcellence in your pursuits by starting with a simple exercise. First, list all of the skills and conditions that could potentially influence your performance at your activity. List every single attribute under your control that you would need to improve on to become exceptional. Don't just list the things that you can personally practice, but also include the environment or the tools that will help you become successful. No matter how trivial, if it can help, add it to your list. If your list has five or six items, it is probably not detailed enough. If it has 15 to 20 items or more, then you are headed in the right direction.

Next, rate yourself in each of these areas on a scale from 1 to 5, where 1 indicates a big area of weakness and 5 indicates a significant advantage. You have to be realistic about how you rate yourself; don't be too harsh or too soft. And remember, this is based on *your* abilities and not based on the skills of someone you admire or someone you see on TV. A good way to do this is to compare yourself with your peers or others at your level of ability. As you perform this exercise, a picture will start to emerge that shows you the micro areas where you need to improve. The goal is to get to as many 5s as you can. When you achieve 4s and 5s on the majority of the items on your list, you will find that your peer group is different because you are performing at a significantly higher level. At this point, redo the exercise.

Create a new list of the 20 or more attributes you need to make yourself excellent. This list may have items that are different from the first, but that is okay because you need a different set of abilities to perform at a higher level. Once again, rate yourself on a scale of 1 to 5. Since your peer group is new and operates at a higher level, you will initially find yourself with a lower score in several categories. Keep improving every little area, one at a time, until you find yourself getting a better score relative to this new set of peers.

This exercise is most effective if you do it in conjunction with your improvement community. Working with those you trust and those who are fully committed to your success will help you create an inclusive list of the attributes you need for success and also help with assigning an objective score to each.

Microexcellence is the stepping-stone to making the most of your talents and becoming exceptional. As with every other element of excellence, it separates the great from the good.

7

FORGET ABOUT YOUR PLAN B

Singer-songwriter Ed Sheeran has sold some 150 million records worldwide, making him one of the world's best-selling recording artists—well before the age of 30. Fans croon his folksy songs in hundreds of millions of showers around the world. Like many exceptionals, Sheeran's immense talent was apparent at a young age and he released his first album when he was barely 14. As a teenager, he was so committed to his music that he believed that every day he did not practice, perform or write a song was a day wasted.[21]

Sheeran knew deep inside himself that all he wanted was to become an extraordinary musician, and he was entirely committed to achieving his dreams. Even if it meant spending his days busking, playing on the streets

---

[21]George Chesterton, 'How Ed Sheeran Became the Biggest Male Popstar on the Planet,' *GQ*, 2 February 2017, https://www.gqmagazine.co.uk/article/ed-sheeran-new-album-divide. Accessed on 1 August 2020.

for small change, and spending his nights often looking for a place to sleep, nothing could change the unwavering commitment to getting better at his craft and becoming a successful artist.

The benefit of not having a place to sleep meant there was no home for him to go back to at the end of the day. Since he lacked other commitments in his life, except for his music, he simply used the extra time to practice, write songs, and interact with and learn from different people every day. All he did was write and perform songs. There was no backup plan or day job or safety net. There was no plan B.

Full commitment toward a single goal worked for him, and Sheeran believes that it could work for anyone, saying, 'Never give yourself a plan B because if you have no backup, there is no possible way you can fail. You'll just go at it [until] it works.'[22] As he got better, he played in front of increasingly larger crowds and his music increased in popularity until he became a household name.

Something that started with such a total commitment resulted in the creation of one of the most successful musical careers of all time. Ed Sheeran is not alone. Every exceptional has felt the same way about achieving their dreams. They have all had a total and unwavering dedication

[22]Aastha Atray Banan, 'Never Give Yourself a Plan B Advises Lego House Singer Ed Sheeran.' *Hindustan Times*, 7 March 2015, https://www.hindustantimes.com/brunch/never-give-your- self-a-plan-b-advices-lego-house-singer-ed-sheeran/storyWePkdm8RY10ECtEWJrRJMO.html. Accessed on 1 August 2020.

to their activity. They went all in to pursue their dreams and without a backup plan. This single-minded focus is a critical component of becoming exceptional.

SINGLE-MINDED FOCUS

When you are wholly committed to a goal and have an unwavering focus to achieve it, good things will happen that will help you realize the goal. As the adage goes, when you want something, the universe conspires in helping you to achieve it. You will see ideas and solutions everywhere, even where you least expect them. Total commitment primes you for achieving your goal; everything you see around you is a catalyst that moves you closer to that end.

The exceptionals know very early on what they want to achieve and they fully commit themselves to attaining it. They often have no idea what else they could have done in their lives. When you fully immerse yourself in trying to be the best in the world in your field, you never think about an alternative. Having a plan B may be the safe and prudent thing to do, but it also reduces your determination to achieve plan A. If you have no safeguard, there's no choice but to succeed.

Plan B, by definition, is the safety net designed to let you attempt to soar as high as you possibly can and reach for that mystical star that you want so badly, but be there to catch you in case you are unable to reach it and fall. Unfortunately, for most people, plan B does exactly the opposite: It prevents them from stretching out and reaching their highest heights.

This is because reaching that magical star is not easy. It requires an enormous amount of will, determination and hard work. Having a safe alternative prevents you from putting in the effort required. When things get tough, as they invariably do, it is easy to give up on your dreams and become naturally drawn to the comfort of your plan B. Exceptionals don't have a plan B because they have focused all of their efforts on achieving plan A.

CLARITY LEADS TO COMMITMENT

Most people are unable to think two or four years ahead, let alone 15 to 20 years ahead. They are so focused on life today that they lack clarity on where they want to go in the long term. As a result, they just go with the tide and simply float around, achieving varying degrees of accomplishments. When you can't articulate what you want from your life, when you lack clarity of purpose, there is little chance for achieving excellence.

Kobe Bryant, one of the most exceptional basketball players of all time, as a child set the specific goal of winning eight NBA championships.[23] He was always crystal clear in his mind about what he wanted. He wanted to win two more championships than his idol Michael Jordan.

---

[23]Joe Rodgers, 'Kobe Bryant: "I Wanted Eight Championships".' *Sporting News*, 2 December 2015, https://www.sportingnews.com/us/nba/news/kobe-bryant-retirement-tour-eight-nba-championships-records-states-mvps-all-star-games/1q4sz4ovgoed1il18ddc9jwhc. Accessed on 1 August 2020.

When Bryant went to the NBA directly from high school, this clarity removed any doubt or second-guessing around his decision to skip college. He knew he wanted to become one of the all-time greats and knew he was headed for superstardom. He was fully committed. As a result, he had an intense and unmatched work ethic that pushed him closer to his goal. While Bryant never achieved the eight championships goal he set for himself—he had to settle for five—the mark he left on the game is indelible.

A lack of clarity results in confusion, frustration, poor performance and efforts that go nowhere. How can you get anywhere when you don't know where you are going? Every exceptional individual knew what they wanted to achieve and the steps they would take to get there. Sometimes things don't work out as planned, but exceptionals are always ready to pivot and either find a new path to their goal or, in some cases, achieve something new, but equally outstanding.

BECOME FUTURE-ORIENTED

The exceptionals are able to remain committed to attaining their goals because they share a future orientation, or the ability to put more weight into decisions that affect their future more than their present. As a result, they are able to set long-term targets and plan the activities that are required to achieve them. They can ward off immediate distractions and become fully dedicated to accomplishing what they set out to do, despite any obstacles they come across. These individuals are very different from those who are present-oriented—who live for the moment, want immediate gratification and quickly give in to temptations.

Unlike present orientation, future orientation means giving up lesser but immediate goals, in favour of larger but later goals. Present-oriented individuals, or those less likely to delay their gratification, are more likely to exhibit impulsive behaviour, which prevents them from sticking to a plan for their future.

Long-term success always goes to the ones who delay their gratification to the future, because they know that the longer-term rewards are far greater than anything they can achieve today. The exceptionals set a long-term goal and go all out toward achieving it and don't deviate from it. Attaining their lofty goals is the only thing they truly wish to achieve. Giving up immediate pleasure for something down the road may appear hard, but there are techniques that can help.

SET THE GOAL, BUT FOCUS ON THE PROCESS

Victorian-era British author Anthony Trollope lived in a time when the physical act of putting pen to paper was the only way to write. In less than 40 years, Trollope wrote 47 novels, two plays, many short stories, travel books and articles. He did that by creating a process for himself and unwaveringly following it.[24]

Trollope believed writing is nothing but turning time

---

[24]'Anthony Trollope.' *British Library*, https://www.bl.uk/people/anthony-trollope#. Accessed on 1 August 2020.

into language, so he decided to focus on setting aside the time to write, knowing that if he did that, the words would follow. He committed to writing from 5:30 a.m. to 8:30 a.m. He even paid his servant an extra fee to get him out of bed by 5:30 with a cup of coffee. That was his process and the commitment he showed to his process resulted in one of the most extraordinary writing feats by an author.[25]

That sort of dedicated focus on a process has played a role in the achievements of anyone who has attained something extraordinary. If you focus on the routine or daily method you go through on your way to achieve your goals, the outcome takes care of itself. For Trollope, it was turning time into words for three hours a day, every single day.

While having a clear goal is essential, remember that the act of setting goals is easy. Everyone has the same goals and everybody dreams about achieving the highest level of success. But only the rarest of people attain them. Those who reach their goals separate themselves from everyone else by committing to a process that works for them.

Your process could be time-based—for example, doing something for a certain number of hours a day. Or it could be activity-based—completing a set of specific tasks every day—or it could be process-based—first, you do *X*, then you move on to *Y*. You could even have a milestone-based approach: work on a task until you can attain something specific. It could be anything that works for you. But without

---

[25]Adam Gopnik, 'Trollope Trending: Why He's Still the Novelist of the Way We Live Now.' *The New Yorker*, 27 April 2015, https://www.newyorker. com/magazine/2015/05/04/trol- lope-trending. Accessed on 1 August 2020.

an ongoing and repeatable technique that keeps moving you ahead, you will not achieve your goals. An easy way to start is to give yourself a daily target for what you want to accomplish every day and stay true to it. No zero days, or days when you do nothing toward your goal.

When I decided to become a writer and was working on my first book, *The Innovation Biome*, I set a milestone-based goal. My target was to write 1,000 words a day. Some days, I wrote more, and some days I wrote a bit less, but that was my daily milestone. Some days I had to think hard about what I wanted to write, and on other days, the writing came easy. Some days, I had to delete what I spent the previous day writing. But that was all okay. It did not have to be perfect. Even though I knew I wanted to produce a high-quality and informative book, I did not focus on the result; I simply committed to writing 1,000 words every day. Before I knew it, I had a finished manuscript. I believe that it was this process that led me to complete my first book, which became a number one bestseller and launched my new career.

Publishing two books is a good accomplishment for me, but is by no means exceptional in the world of writing. Consider Ian Fleming, the prolific writer who brought James Bond to the world. Fleming meets every criterion of being extraordinary in his profession as a writer. He not only created an iconic character but also a wealth of unmistakably unique personalities and adventures that have resonated with our imagination for decades. Very few writers have created a world that we all know as well as the world of James Bond.

Fleming started to write at a relatively late stage in his life. He was 44 when he started to work on his first book, *Casino Royale*. He was fortunate to be able to draw from his prior experiences serving as an officer in the British Naval Intelligence Department and also from his natural gift of having a vivid imagination. But in creating the James Bond series, he knew that imagination and experience alone were not enough. He would need to go through the process of writing an entire book, and the thought of writing 300 pages was daunting. He needed a routine that worked for him.

Similar to Trollope's approach, Fleming set aside time every day to write. He would write each morning from 9:30 a.m. to 12:30 p.m. and then for another hour in the evening between 6:00 p.m. and 7:00 p.m. He spent four hours a day writing. That was it. At the end of the four hours, he would number all of the typewritten pages, put them away, and celebrate a productive day much in the manner Bond would have done.

As part of his process, Fleming would never go back and correct himself as he wrote. He wouldn't check to see if his ideas flowed, whether his work was readable or even to check a spelling or validate a fact. All of that could wait until after there was a complete manuscript. He stuck to this method, which yielded him 2,000 words a day, and within six weeks, a new James Bond novel was born.[26]

---

[26]Emily Temple, 'Ian Fleming Explains How to Write a Thriller.' *Literary Hub*, 28 May 2019, https://lithub.com/ian-fleming-explains-how-to-write-a-thriller. Accessed on 1 August 2020.

Like Trollope and Fleming, every exceptional has used a process that works best for them and has stayed committed to it. Your best bet to achieve new heights is to find the approach that works well for what you are trying to accomplish. Once you establish your process and consistently remain committed to it, you will soon find yourself realizing goals you never thought were within your reach.

USE A COMMITMENT DEVICE

Now that we understand that the most successful people observe a set process, we also need to realize that for most people, committing to a routine is challenging and takes a lot of discipline. Consequently, they give up. It is hard to stay motivated and remain committed, and it is especially hard to stay focused when you have your phone next to you, screaming for your attention every few minutes. It is hard to be persistent and follow through on a monotonous routine every single day, particularly when you don't see visible progress early in the process.

When things are difficult, we tend to stop doing them. Why should we keep pushing ourselves so hard to achieve something so distant? But not giving up and staying true to the process separate those who achieve their dreams from those who don't. As we've discussed, commitments are hard to keep because there is an ongoing battle between the present and the future, an inherent conflict between what we know is good for us in the long term versus what we want to do right now. For the exceptionals, who have a high degree of self-control, the future always wins (future orientation). For others, who succumb to gratifying their immediate needs, the present comes out victorious (present orientation).

We have engaged in this battle a million times. For example, we know that we want to get that promotion at work, make the select team in our sport, complete an Ironman triathlon or write a book. We know each of these is a long-term commitment that will require effort and sacrifice.

Fighting these long-term commitments is the immediate desire that prevents us from attaining what we know is good for us. For example, we get caught up in thoughts like 'It's raining, and I feel like sleeping in instead of training,' or 'I want to go out with my friends rather than complete the assignment at work'.

As illogical as it sounds, even though we know what is good for us, we consciously select an alternative that we know goes against us attaining our goals. But we do it because it is hard to always think about a future that is years or decades out. We give in to our immediate desires because they are more tangible, more satisfying and are instantly gratifying.

The exceptionals have the discipline to resist immediate temptations and keep their eyes on the long-term prize. If you have trouble prioritizing long-term gain over short-term desire, there is a tool you can use to force yourself to not give in to your immediate desires. The tool, called a *commitment device*, removes the temptation and sometimes punishes you in some way for not doing what you know you should be doing.

When I need to concentrate on my research and writing, I put my phone in a different room. That way, I can focus on what I know I should be doing. When my mind begins to wander and I absently reach out for it and realize it is not there, I remember I put it away for a reason. Putting my phone away in another room is a commitment device.

Cutting up your credit card is a commitment device that prevents you from spending money needlessly. Or perhaps you decide that if you don't practice your activity for two hours a day, you will donate 20 dollars to a charity or household fund. Handing over the cash is one way to keep you motivated. A common and useful commitment device is practicing or working with a partner or a coach. You can't take the day off if you know someone else is there waiting for you. There are countless commitment devices that you can establish for yourself or those around you. You have to pick one to help you stay true to your daily process, and it is this adherence to your simple routine that will vault you to achieving incredible heights.

Commitment devices have been responsible for some of the most famous feats in human history. The acclaimed author, playwright and poet Victor Hugo is one prominent example. In 1830, Hugo continually found himself distracted and tempted to go out every evening and socialize rather than focus on his writing. He knew he needed to hunker down and work, so later that year, he created his commitment device: He locked away his formal clothes, so he had nothing to wear at evening soirees. He bought himself a bottle of ink and a grey shawl that he wore every day.

Hugo put himself in a situation where he could do nothing else but write. So that was all he did, and in January 1831, his masterpiece, *The Hunchback of Notre Dame*, was born. His commitment device, which was to not have access to his evening wear, forced him to stick to his routine. Once he did that, he was able to produce exceptional work that has been at the forefront of the literary world for centuries.

GOAL WRITING BEATS GOAL THINKING

We know goal setting is essential, and we know that we need to stay committed to our goals. But our best bet to achieve our goals is the simple act of writing them down, instead of simply leaving them in our minds. The act of writing down something gives you a stronger connection with your goal. Studies have shown that people who establish goals and then write them down accomplish significantly more than others who set the same goals but do not write them down.[27]

When you write down your goals, you make neural connections in your mind which don't occur when you merely think about your goals. By making your goals tangible, you form a bond between what you want to achieve

---

[27]'Goals Research Summary.' *Dominican University of California*, https://www.dominican.   edu/sites/default/files/2020-02/gailmatthews-harvard-goals-researchsummary.pdf. Accessed on 1 August 2020.

and the energy you put into it.

Very few people in the world have worked harder to attain incredible goals than the most decorated Olympian in the world, Michael Phelps, whose focus on 'microexcellence' was discussed earlier in the book. Phelps consistently pushed the limits of human abilities with his intense training sessions and he epitomized the concept of no zero days. He believed that if you took a day off from swimming, it would take you two days to get back what you lost during that single day off. At one point, over a period of seven years, he had spent only five days without getting in the water. He had 10 workouts every week and was swimming approximately seven miles a day for 365 days of the year. Despite the immense talent he was born with, there was simply no one who outworked Phelps.

But Phelps knew precisely why he put himself through these gruelling training sessions. He would write down his goals on a piece of paper, so they were there to remind him why he was working so hard. Like everybody else, there were days when Phelps did not want to get out of bed for yet another brutal workout. On those days, he would look at the piece of paper on which he had written his goals for a reminder of why he needed to work, and he would get back in the pool for another intense session.[28]

---

[28]Emmie Martin, '23-time Gold Medalist Michael Phelps Uses a Simple Trick to Stay Focused on His Goals.' *CNBC*, 1 January 2019, https://www.cnbc.com/2018/12/20/michael-phelps-strategy-for-reaching-his-goals.html. Accessed on 1 August 2020.

ACTUALLY DO IT

Have you written down your goals? Most likely, you have not. Maybe you think writing down your goals is a silly exercise, one that you hear about frequently but that you can pass on. You know what you are striving to achieve and that is all you need. But to become exceptional, you need to take the time to write your goals down as this gives you a level of clarity, introspection and commitment that you otherwise can't get. The act of writing down your goals becomes a pledge to yourself and creates a tighter connection between what you desire and what you will do to achieve it. Most of the greats that you admire have done this.

Your goals need to be very explicit—the more specific, the better. You need to state exactly what you want to achieve, along with a specific timeframe for achieving each thing. You also need to be very clear about the effort you are willing to put into your goal attainment, and you need to have a strategy that you are willing to follow. Just taking the time to write down your detailed goals in this manner will serve as a valuable exercise to gain clarity about what you want and to understand what you are willing to do.

For inspiration and ideas, here is what Bruce Lee, the most exceptional martial artist the world has ever seen, wrote down in 1969:

'I, Bruce Lee, will be the highest-paid Oriental superstar in the United States. In return, I will give the most exciting performances and render the best of quality in the capacity of an actor. Starting in 1970, I will achieve world fame, and from then onward till the end of 1980, I will have in my possession the sum of $10,000,000. Then I will live the way I please and achieve inner harmony and happiness.'[29]

EXPANDING PLAN A

Joan Benoit Samuelson, the renowned Olympic gold-medal marathoner, did not plan on being a runner. Her dream was to represent the US Olympic team as a skier. When she was 15 years old, she suffered a ski accident that ended in a broken leg, and as a result, she took up running to help with her rehabilitation.

The accident derailed her dream of becoming an elite skier. But she had learnt the qualities of what it takes to become exceptional. Soon, running became her sport, and she was able to apply everything she had learnt to become one of the best marathoners the world had ever seen. Just seven years after picking up running, she entered the Boston Marathon as a complete unknown and won the race, shattering the course record by eight minutes.

Paradoxically, the act of being fully committed to something—of not having a plan B—can open up multiple alternative paths—maybe not plan A but something you couldn't have predicted enough to make into a plan B. Samuelson's clarity and commitment to becoming a world-

---

[29]'Think, Grow Rich, or Die Trying: The Bruce Lee Story.' *Martial Development*, https:// www.martialdevelopment.com/think-grow-rich-or-die-trying-the-bruce-lee-story. Accessed on 1 August 2020.

class skier opened up avenues she never expected. While she never had a plan B, an exceptional career in running became a new plan A.

Sometimes, things are out of your control. You may try to become the very best in the world at something, and despite your considerable efforts, you may not get there. However, the traits you picked up while you were trying to become the best can help you succeed in other areas because they are transferrable. Many people who did not achieve their dream of becoming professional athletes or musicians, despite their best efforts, have gone on to become successful entrepreneurs, lawyers, doctors or leaders in the community. Their desire, dedication, discipline, ability to learn and improve and all of the other desirable qualities they have developed over the years have translated to success in other fields. And despite not achieving their original dream, these people have found happy, fulfilled, productive and successful lives.

Your best plan B is not having one. If you put all of your energy into becoming your possible best, you have a good chance of achieving your very lofty goals. And even if you don't, you still will have learned the skill sets that are necessary to attain success. You will be able to apply these skills to a different field, and that is what being exceptional is all about.

INTENSE EFFORT

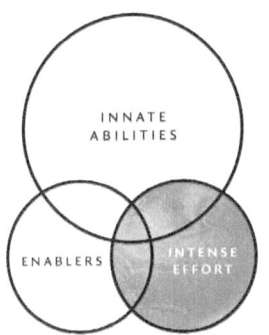

INNATE
ABILITIES

ENABLERS

INTENSE
EFFORT

8

NO ONE WILL OUTWORK ME

The separation is in the preparation. Most of us have heard this phrase, and it is often used as motivation by coaches trying to get the best effort and results from their teams. The meaning of this phrase is simple: Without effort, hard work and skill development, you are unlikely to achieve success. Of course, we know that. But it is important to remember that this is true and is often the difference between those who excel and those who don't.

There is no question that you need to have a set of innate abilities to become outstanding. As we have already discussed, the traits you are born with and can thank your parents for are foundational to becoming exceptional. Your genes account for 50 per cent of your performance. But your innate characteristics only serve to get you in the door that is reserved for the most elite. Once you're there, every other aspect of your eventual success depends on acquired characteristics, of which effort, dedicated practice and focused skill development are the chief influencers.

Pop sensation Justin Bieber, who is always around thousands of screaming and adoring fans, became a worldwide icon through an intense work ethic. He is considered one of the hardest-working stars in music and has been from day one. Just like every exceptional, he was born with an innate gift for music. His immense talent was apparent at a young age. But it was his relentless toiling that helped him expose that vast talent to the world. Hard work was his separation and advantage over anyone else who may have been born with just as much raw talent.

As Bieber tried to make his mark, most record companies rejected him. But that did not deter him. He would play for anyone who would listen. No audience was too small. He played at parks, shopping malls and busked on the streets. He visited just about every radio station in the country that would let him play, and he played anywhere and everywhere, without an ego, solely with the desire to work as hard as was necessary and be heard.[30]

As he kept playing and getting more practice and more repetitions, he kept improving. And as he got better, his audiences started to get larger, until he transitioned from being good to great and eventually reaching exceptional.

The amount of time you spend on an activity is a critical determinant of your ultimate success. While practicing

---

[30]Peter Sheridan, 'Justin Bieber: The World's Hardest-Working Heart-Throb.' *Daily Express*, 19 February 2011, https://www.express.co.uk/expressyourself/229987/Justin-Bieber-The- world-s-hardest-working-heart-throb. Accessed on 1 August 2020.

something for, say, 10,000 hours may be a noteworthy milestone, that is just the start. Volume, or the number of hours honing a skill set, is irreplaceable. The exceptionals have invested decades into honing their skills. You need to do the same, if only because you never get back a lost day or a lost minute.

Intense effort, deliberate practice and plain old hard work are necessary components of becoming exceptional; there is no escaping it. The majority of the world's inspirational quotes are about the benefits of working hard. Every exceptional has put in the immense amount of energy required for enhancing their skills and reaching the top. They have all made sacrifices, paid their dues and struggled through pain. They have, quite frankly, outworked everyone around them.

FORTY HOURS ISN'T NEARLY ENOUGH

Becoming exceptional is not a 40-hours-a-week job; it requires a total and absolute commitment. You need to be working on or thinking about your cause all the time. You need to have an unmatched work ethic; you can't take evenings and weekends off. You have to be prepared to immerse yourself in improving your skills.

The common thread across all of the most exceptional individuals is that every single one of them has invested an inordinate amount of volume and an unmatched amount of work to achieve their success. Yes, they were all born with talent, and yes, they were in an environment that brought out their best. But no one was able to outwork them.

The exceptional entertainer and actor Will Smith insists that the separation between him and anybody else is his 'ridiculous' and 'sickening' work ethic. He will put in whatever effort it takes, even if it kills him. As an example, if he goes up against anyone else to see who can last longer on a treadmill, he believes there are only two options: Either the other person will get off or Smith will die trying.[31] There is no way he will let anyone else outwork him. While Smith's example may appear to be an extreme obsession with hard work, his sentiment is shared by every exceptional. No one will outwork them, and no one has worked with more intensity.

Even if you are gifted with an insane amount of talent and are born to be a sprinter like Usain Bolt, a swimmer like Michael Phelps, a tennis ace like Serena Williams, a golfer like Tiger Woods, a basketball player like Michael Jordan or a business icon like Bill Gates or Elon Musk, the fundamental requirement to fulfil your potential is hard work. Every Nobel laureate has dedicated all of their waking hours to trying to solve problems that propel humanity forward. Without exception, each person who has scaled their pyramid has their own story about the immense effort they devoted to get to the top.

Are you willing to do the same?

---

[31]'Will Smith: Talent vs. Hard Work.' *YouTube*, https://www.youtube.com/watch?v=05nO- roFYIF8. Accessed on 1 August 2020.

WORKING HARD IS HARD BUT SATISFYING

Working hard is incredibly hard. Very few people have the discipline to put in the effort and energy, day after day and year after year, to get better at their craft, especially at a time when the bar to excellence keeps rising and the level of competency required to become outstanding is also getting higher and higher. To become the best, you have to maximize your full potential, take advantage of every resource available to you and attain your possible best. The only way you can do that is by pushing yourself in a way you could never imagine.

Some people are simply more motivated and naturally harder workers than others. They can put in the conscious and dedicated effort because they have a clear goal, and they know the only way to achieve it is through hard work. You know who these people are; you see them around you all the time. They are the ones who are the most diligent about putting in the effort required for every task because they know they want to do it well. These are the people who end up rising to the top.

Most people have the desire to work hard but lack the spark to get going, the tools to stay motivated or the willingness to grind through, especially when early results of their labour are not apparent. But the good news is that anyone can develop the ability to work hard, and once you learn how, the feeling of working hard can be rewarding and deeply satisfying.

Very few things beat the sensation of knowing you have

given everything you have to your current task. Whether you achieve the outcomes you are aiming for or not, merely the act of applying every bit of your abilities is gratifying. It provides you with a positive feedback loop that keeps you motivated to work even harder.

Imagine you could somehow convince yourself to get up and work harder than you ever have. Imagine that you could relentlessly focus on developing your skills and not get distracted by anything else. What would you be able to achieve? If you maximized your potential, could you become among the best at what you do? Wouldn't you like to know how far you can go? Why does being exceptional have to be reserved for someone else? Why can't it be you?

With the right level of motivation, you can work as hard as you need to. Unlike the genes you are born with or the environment that nurtures you, the energy you expend is one factor that is entirely under your control. You decide how you spend your time—you can spend it sharpening your skills or doing something less rewarding. There is no secret to working hard; you just have to do it.

DELIBERATE PRACTICE ACCOUNTS FOR 25 PER CENT OF EXCEPTIONAL OUTCOMES

How much effort is required to become the very best? The short answer is that you need to put in more effort than everyone else. Your metric should be to work harder than anyone you see around you who is eyeing the same goal. If someone is practicing for four hours a day, you need to practice for five, and you need to ensure that the five hours you practice are deliberate and productive. If your co-workers are working nine hours a day, you may need to put in ten, and again, your efforts need to be thoughtful and deliberate in learning new skills and sharpening existing ones. Spending time going through the motions is a waste.

Over the past few decades, thousands of studies have attempted to examine the link between deliberate practice and performance. Researchers around the world have tried to quantify this link in fields spanning sport, music, games, education and a host of other professions. One meta-analysis (a scientific review of existing research) of this topic showed that deliberate practice accounts for a substantial amount of the variation in outcomes across a range of professions. In categories where the volume of effort could be accurately measured (e.g., games, sport, or music), the analysis found that deliberate practice accounted for approximately 20 per cent to 25 per cent of the variation in performance.[32]

The game of *Scrabble* is played on millions of kitchen tables around the world. While most of us associate a prolific vocabulary with success at the game and covet the opportunity to place a tile on a 'triple-word-score' square, that's not how the best *Scrabble* players in the world play it. At the elite level, *Scrabble* is a different game altogether.

---

[32]Brooke N. Macnamara, D. Z. Hambrick, and F. L. Oswald, 'Deliberate Practice and Performance in Music, Games, Sports, Education, and Professions: A Meta-Analysis.' *Psychological Science* (2014), doi: 10.1177/0956797614535810.

It is no longer a game of words; it is partly a game of math and partly a test of spatial aptitude, or the ability to use letter combinations with existing openings on the board. But most important, competitive *Scrabble* is a game of memory. It is about a player's ability to commit to memory the *Scrabble* dictionary, something that only happens with intense effort and practice. An elite *Scrabble* player will have memorized about 100,000 words—a significant portion of the *Scrabble* dictionary.

New Zealander Nigel Richards may not be a household name, but he is in a class by himself at *Scrabble*. He is the Michael Jordan of the game, with an enviable record of winning the *Scrabble* world championship five times and winning dozens of notable tournaments around the world. However, perhaps Richards's most remarkable achievement was winning the French-language *Scrabble* championship even though he didn't even speak the language. He created French words on the board not knowing what they meant. He did it by effectively memorizing the French dictionary, an act that requires intense and concentrated practice and effort.[33]

In games such as *Scrabble*, chess or even *Jeopardy*, it is easy to measure a direct link between practice and performance. The champions in these events are invariably the ones who have worked the hardest and are most

---

[33]Kim Willsher, 'The French Scrabble Champion Who Doesn't Speak French.' *The Guardian*, 21 July 2015, https://www.theguardian.com/lifeandstyle/2015/jul/21/new-french-scrabble- champion-nigel-richards-doesnt-speak-french. Accessed on 1 August 2020.

prepared. The same is true for many other domains, like athletics or piano recitals, or even for the grades you get on an exam. There is a directly observable link between effort and results.

In other fields, it may be harder to isolate what specific activities constitute practice. But the same principles hold true in your profession or craft, whatever it may be. Practice still makes perfect.

GET COMFORTABLE BEING UNCOMFORTABLE

Pushing yourself hard means getting out of your comfort zone, something that is difficult for many of us to do. To reach the highest heights you have to get comfortable with stretching your abilities and pushing yourself to physically, mentally and emotionally operate at a level that is beyond what you are accustomed to.

As humans, we function at our optimal level when we have a moderate degree of anxiety or are slightly outside our comfort zone. If we have no apprehension or remain fully within our comfort zone, we don't push ourselves and, consequently, don't achieve something spectacular. On the other hand, in situations where we are too far out of our comfort zone, we become unproductive because unusually high anxiety causes stress that can hurt our performance. To strive for the extraordinary, we have to learn to push ourselves to operate comfortably outside our comfort zone.

Holding your breath underwater for an extended period is one of the most uncomfortable things you can try. Most of us can do it for maybe a minute, perhaps a little longer. Then we feel the distressing sensation of our lungs exploding and our bodies craving air and urgently shooting us up to the surface as quickly as possible.

Unlike most of us, Aleix Segura of Spain has held his breath underwater for 24 minutes and has held the Guinness World Record for static apnoea (floating in a pool and holding one's breath for as long as possible). Twenty-four minutes! Think about it. That is longer than the time it would take me to drive out for an ice cream cone, sample a few, select one and drive back home—all while Segura hasn't taken a single breath.

You simply can't pull off such a feat unless you are comfortable being uncomfortable. You, too, will need to subject yourself to a similar level of discomfort to become elite in your field and be willing to endure the agony and anguish it brings. Segura pushed himself to the limits to accomplish his remarkable achievements. But even for a champion like him, the anxiety of a tournament prevents him from doing his best. He has held his breath for longer during his training sessions, when he was able to operate at his optimal level of stress.[34]

To achieve new heights, we need to maintain our optimal anxiety level by pushing ourselves hard enough to be able to handle uncomfortable situations, but not so far

---

[34]Robbie Gonzalez, 'What It Takes to Hold Your Breath for 24 Minutes (Yeah, It's a Thing).' *Wired*, 24 August 2017, https://www.wired.com/story/what-it-takes-to-hold-your-breath- for-24-minutes-yeah-its-a-thing. Accessed on 1 August 2020.

as to let the discomfort overwhelm our performance. That is the zone we want to be in to determine if our efforts are going to be productive. But remember that humans are physiologically and psychologically resilient. We can push ourselves quite hard to attain new limits, and that is why every generation keeps advancing over the ones before.

Pushing yourself until you are in a moderately uncomfortable situation allows you to get used to the feeling of discomfort that comes with hard work. That is the level of exertion you need to invest in growing your skills and learning new ones. Challenge yourself hard enough to raise your level of unease but not so much that you give up. Doing so will allow you to experience sensations you have never felt before and will help you become more accepting of the rigors of hard work.

You can get better at pushing yourself out of your comfort zone the same way you get better at anything else: with practice. Practice pushing yourself by putting in longer, more concentrated hours, learning new skills and making your improvement efforts deliberate.

Another way to get out of your comfort zone is by doing something new. Take on a new skill, something you have never done, and do it until you feel comfortable with it. The journey from novice to proficient, even in small activities, gives you the feeling of pushing yourself and the sensation of moving from distress to comfort. As you learn newer skills, you will not only become more comfortable with discomfort, but your improvements will start occurring at an accelerated pace.

Task immersion can also help you get used to the sensation of pushing yourself. When we do something, we often get distracted by looking at the clock to see when we can be done with our practice or work. Time is the wrong metric for determining effort. Put your clock away and immerse yourself fully into the task. If you take away the element of time and focus purely on skill development, you are more likely to push yourself harder and more efficiently.

INCREASING YOUR TOLERANCE FOR PAIN

Hard work induces pain. Not just physical pain but a host of sensations, including mental fatigue and discomfort that make us want to give up and quit. It is usually the primary reason why we don't achieve more in our lives. Hard work is painful and there is no escaping that. But the human body and mind are remarkable at adapting to pain, and your overall pain threshold can be altered.

One technique is to exercise regularly. Exercise truly is a panacea, and you can add pain tolerance to the list of exercise's countless benefits. Research in the area has shown that moderate to intense exercise or aerobic training can increase a person's psychological pain tolerance.

When you exercise, your pain threshold does not change, which means you are still susceptible to pain and will feel the same amount you have always felt. But even as exercise strengthens the parts of the body you train, it also alters how your mind perceives pain and therefore applies to your ability to tolerate discomfort across a range of activities and professions. Regardless of the domain you wish to excel at, adding exercise to your daily routine will allow you to push yourself harder.

The more you exercise, the more your tolerance to pain increases, and you can sustain unpleasant activities for a longer time. As a result, people who exercise regularly become more unflappable because they can better tolerate the discomfort that comes with hard work. When you can endure more pain, you can work harder at anything. The ability to bear a higher degree of mental and physical distress enables you to improve your skills most effectively.[35]

Individual tolerance to pain is like a bell curve, where a few people have an incredibly high resistance and a few people have a very low tolerance. Most of the population is somewhere in the middle. So, if you find yourself lacking the self-motivation to put in the hard work you need, adding exercise to your routine can gradually move you further along the curve of increased pain tolerance and, consequently, increase your ability to work harder.

As your ability to withstand pain increases, so does your ability to put in more effort, and soon, you start to see the fruits of your labour. Exercise appears to be one of the few common elements shared by everyone who has achieved excellence in any field. Just about every exceptional seems to start their day, no matter how demanding, with exercise.

---

[35]Gretchen Reynolds, 'How Exercise Helps Us Tolerate Pain.' *The New York Times*, 13 August 2014, https://well.blogs.nytimes.com/2014/08/13/how-exercise-helps-us-tolerate-pain. Accessed on 1 August 2020.

FAILURE TO CONNECT WITH YOUR FUTURE SELF

One reason people don't put in the effort to invest in themselves is because they feel disconnected from who they will be in the future. They think of their future self as another person—a stranger or, at best, a distant relative. And while people are more willing to make sacrifices for themselves or the people closest to them, they will not make sacrifices for those with whom they don't feel a bond. Since they feel detached from their future self, they do not take the actions today that will benefit them later on in their life. The decisions they make today fail to put them in a position to achieve exceptional results tomorrow.

Hal Hershfield, social psychologist at the Anderson School of Management, University of California, Los Angeles (UCLA), has been studying the phenomenon of the future self. His experiments involve connecting the present self with the future self. Participants in his research studies were shown virtual-reality images of how they would appear when they got older. They were allowed to interact and spend some time with their older virtual-reality doppelgängers. The intention was to let them connect their present and future selves at a very personal and visceral level.

Once participants established a bond with their future selves, they were increasingly more vested in making the right decisions for their future. They were more willing to make sacrifices today and forgo immediate rewards to invest in themselves in the future. In other words, once they felt more connected with their future selves, they were willing to adopt short-term pain for long-term gains.[36]

Only if you believe that the long-term gains are valuable will you be willing to invest the energy necessary to achieve them. Tools similar to Hershfield's research can help connect you to your future self.

It's jarring to take a long hard look at an image of what you will look like at a later age. It is eye-opening. There are apps you can download where you use any photo of yourself, and within a few seconds, you see yourself as an older person, having aged a few decades. Go through this exercise and spend a few minutes connecting with your future self. Ask yourself what your life will be like when you look like the person in the image. Establishing a bond with an older and greyer version of yourself may not be a pleasant experience, but it can serve as a motivational prompt to get you closer to achieving your dreams.

INTENSE EFFORT MEANS AIMING FOR YOUR POSSIBLE BEST

We learn from a very young age that the key to success at anything is hard work. As we mature, we begin to see the definitive link between hard work and results. We understand that effort and persistence are essential elements for sustained excellence. Every person who has reached the top has worked harder than most of us can ever imagine.

---

[36]'Research.' *Hal Hershfield*, www.halhershfield.com/research. Accessed on 1 August 2020.

We know this, yet somehow the ability to put in the intense effort simply escapes most of us. Maybe we are just not as motivated as others. Perhaps we are lazy. Maybe we believe we don't have what it takes to become exceptional, maybe we are afraid of failure or, quite possibly, we are fearful of success.

But if your goal is to become truly exceptional, there is no other way. You have to put in the effort. Hard work means that you need perform a task to the best of your ability and to the exclusion of everything else. It is not just about going through the motions or the number of hours you spend at a task. It is essentially about mastering a skill, showing up and giving it your all.

When you set out to outwork everyone else, your goal should not be to compare your efforts to those of others. You should focus on achieving your possible best every day. That is the only way to improve. It is natural to measure your progress against that of others, and how you measure up against others is often a good yardstick and motivator, but you can't control what others do. You can only control yourself, which is why greatness transcends competition and centres on you. Only through intense effort will you see progress and fresh results. And when you notice the results of your efforts, and like what you see, your motivation and ability to work even harder will increase.

JOINING THE EXCEPTIONALS

9

JOINING THE EXCEPTIONALS

Achieving exceptional status means being part of the rarefied and highly selective club of the most elite. It means being part of the permyriad, the top 1 per cent of the 1 per cent, or one out of every 10,000 people. It means becoming one of the most accomplished 30,000 people in the country, based on the current US population.

To put this number in perspective, fewer than 1,000 Americans have won any kind of medal in the Olympics (summer and winter) over the past 40 years, and there have been fewer than 200 US Nobel laureates during that time. There are currently fewer than 3,000 professional athletes on the rosters of the three major sports leagues in the country (baseball, basketball, and football).

If you believe people shaping the largest corporations are exceptional, then counting the five most accomplished executives from every Fortune 500 company adds another 2,500 people. If you consider the most proficient musicians, entertainers, politicians, artists, athletes in myriad other sports, entrepreneurs, and TV personalities as exceptional, that adds probably another 3,000 people.

All of the groups listed above add up to less than 10,000 people in total. That leaves over 20,000 of the permyriad unaccounted for, and they are the most outstanding achievers in every other field.

You don't have to be a top athlete, entertainer or a household name to join the permyriad club. You could be just as exceptional as a nurse, architect, lawyer, educator, artist, marketer, musician, engineer, salesperson, chef, accountant, doctor, actor, business owner, analyst, writer or anything else.

Every field has room for its own set of ultra-elite members whose achievements are so spectacular that they take our breath away. Anyone willing to make the commitment and do what it takes to become exceptional can enter the permyriad club. As exclusive as the club is, anyone who is willing to excel in their field is welcome.

INSIDE THE MINDS OF THE PERMYRIAD

Reaching an elite level in anything is a remarkable achievement. But even among the elite, a few people stand out as truly one of a kind. They have not only reached the top of their field, but even among the best, they are unique and other elites can't match their accomplishments. These are the super-elite, the rarest of individuals, who have scaled unfathomable heights.

All National Basketball Association players are elite athletes, but then there are Michael Jordan, LeBron James and Kobe Bryant, whose accomplishments stand out as ultra-exceptional. All golfers who play on the PGA Tour are elite, but then there are Tiger Woods and Jack Nicklaus, who stand taller than the rest. All major corporation CEOs are elite, but then there are those like Bill Gates, Elon Musk and Steve Jobs who have impacted society at a different scale altogether. All Olympians are elite, but the performances of Simone Biles, Usain Bolt and Michael Phelps will always stand out. All cricketers who play for the India national cricket team are exceptional, but players like Sachin Tendulkar are cut from a different cloth.

There is a significant difference between the elite and the super-elite. It is not so much in raw domain abilities— the elite and super-elite are just as talented—instead, the difference lies in the psyche and attitude that has let the super-elites strive for, and achieve, so much more.

As discussed in chapter 3, Lew Hardy, Matthew Barlow, Lynne Evans and their colleagues have done some fascinating work that focuses on the differences between the elites and the super-elites.[37] They attempted to understand the minds and circumstances that led to the success of these exceptional individuals, and their research has uncovered insights into some noteworthy factors that drive extreme excellence.

---

[37]Lew Hardy et al., 'Great British Medalists: Psychosocial Biographies of Super-Elite and Elite Athletes from Olympic Sports.' *Progress in Brain Research* 232 (2017): 1–119, doi:10.1016/ bs.pbr.2017.03.004.

They studied 32 world-class athletes, of which 16 were elite athletes, those who reached the most competitive or elite levels in their sport and represented their country at the Olympics or major international events. But they did not medal at the Olympic Games or the world championships.

The other 16 participants were the super-elites. These were individuals who had won at least one gold medal and at least one other medal (either gold or silver) at either the Olympics or the world championships. This put them in a very select group of athletes who are gold medallists and world champions. On average, each super-elite had won six medals in major international competitions, a truly remarkable achievement.

The researchers interviewed the athletes, their parents and coaches across a variety of dimensions to get an accurate and comprehensive picture of the psychosocial factors that made these athletes who they are. While this study includes only athletes, the observations can be applied to other fields to give us a peek into the minds and circumstances of some of the most exceptional individuals in the world.

The first thing we learn is that these exceptionals are no different from anyone else. They have their own set of motivations, high and low points, abilities, struggles and experiences. They have days when they are ready to give up and days when they are motivated to work harder than ever, sometimes to the point of injury.

Both groups of athletes share several common characteristics. They all came from environments that advocated a culture of striving. They grew up in homes where excellence was expected. Also, athletes in both groups experienced positive pivotal moments in their lives that prompted them to push forward in their careers. Both the elite and super-elite athletes exhibited conscientiousness, dedication, and commitment to their sport and their training. And they all demonstrated the factors discussed in this book that are necessary to achieve pre-eminence in any field.

But there was a distinct set of factors that separated the two groups. Unlike the elites, the super-elites went through a significant negative life event, such as the loss of a parent or loved one, parental divorce or an unsettled environment that resulted in substantial trauma in their minds. This gave them a 'chip on their shoulder' or extra motivation to pursue excellence. Often this negative shock was followed closely by a positive experience in their sport that compensated for the loss and served as a catalyst to becoming exceptional.

The super-elites were also more likely to have experienced a critical, pivotal moment in their sport that prompted them to become more determined to excel. In some cases, this pivotal moment was positive, such as meeting a new mentor or coach who had a fresh approach that they latched on to; in other cases, the pivotal moment was negative, such as an injury or a crushing defeat that haunted them and fuelled their desire to work harder. But the set of traits that showed consistent separation between the super-elites and the elites was around an elevated desire to excel and a need to succeed. Becoming the best wasn't merely a desire;

it was a necessity.

Compared to the elites, the super-elites exhibited obsessiveness, selfishness, perfectionism and an unmatched commitment.

They had no time or desire to do anything else except excel in their sport. While the elites sometimes entertained the idea of pursuing other careers over their athletic pursuits, the super-elites never thought of doing anything else and were fully committed. They knew they wanted to excel in their domain, and nothing else entered their mind.

There indeed was no Plan B for the super-elites. They were ruthless in their pursuit of perfection and exhibited a self-centred and unrelenting focus on their goals. While these characteristics may not always be socially acceptable, this need and obsessiveness for achievement and a relentless focus on goals helped them in their pursuit of extreme distinction in their domains. They knew what they wanted and were willing to make any sacrifices necessary.

While the elites wanted to excel and win in their events, they narrowly focused on the outcomes or how they performed relative to others. Super-elites were different. They emphasized mastery in their sport, in addition to the outcomes they achieved. Of course, they cared about the results and wanted to win; that is what competition is all about. But because they wanted to become the best they possibly could, achieving mastery was just as crucial as winning against others. They were always striving to achieve their possible best.

THE THREE STAGES OF EXCELLENCE

Every exceptional journey, from novice to ultra-elite, has transitioned through three stages or degrees of evolution. The three stages of growth are seamless and there is no distinct milestone that separates one from the other, but understanding the progression is helpful as you evaluate your journey. The three stages are *the positive, the comparative,* and *the superlative.*

The Positive Stage

This is the first stage of skill development. You are new to an area. No matter what your domain is, you are learning fundamental new skills. These early experiences need to be enjoyable and positive and should leave you wanting more. Positive outcomes keep you motivated and provide you the energy and joy to keep going. In this stage, you learn whether you have a natural aptitude for an area and whether you are interested in pursuing it.

During this stage, you are usually doing something because of the inherent joy and positive feedback your activity provides and not because you think you can excel at it. Learning is usually fun at this stage. Whether you are a child learning a new activity or a young professional starting in a new field or even a veteran doing something new, you need to start with a positive relationship with your activity where you look forward to participating, learning and improving.

Your primary outcome at this stage is gaining positive experiences.

The Comparative Stage

During this stage, you are committed to your field. You are looking to get better, and you compare yourself to your previous accomplishments or to the achievements of others. Your peers and your past performances become your yardstick and you want to develop a set of skills that matches or exceeds them.

During this stage, you invest in systematic learning and technical skill development. You spend more time trying to improve and perfect your craft with a set of mentors, teachers, or instructors who can help you get better. You focus on the outcomes you have achieved. Your benchmarks at this stage are comparisons with your previous results and how you are doing relative to others. Since we are competitive and comparative by nature, this is the stage where people generally feel most comfortable. Very few people move past this phase.

Your primary outcome at this stage is establishing new personal bests.

The Superlative Stage

This stage is where you enter the realm of true expertise. Your mindset has transcended from comparing yourself to others or achieving more than you previously have to maximizing your potential. At this stage, you are focused on the mastery of your craft and enhancing your abilities purely for yourself and the satisfaction of doing the best you possibly can. While you still require technical assistance and you still need to develop functional skills, your thinking has evolved to become transformational rather than incremental. You focus on the big-picture strategy over technical skill development.

By this point, your capabilities have become whole and you have the functional skills you need to perform at the highest level. Your energy now is less focused on what you achieve relative to others and more on being the best you can be. You know that there may be others who are better than you, and you may not be successful every single time, but your goal is to maximize your potential.

Your primary outcome at this stage is striving for your possible best.

PIVOT POINTS

Very often, the journey to becoming exceptional starts with a spark that uncovers a talent or a desire to excel, or an opportunity to do something special. This spark influences your subsequent actions and motivates you to strive for excellence. The more motivated you are, the more likely you are to become exceptional. The most accomplished people in the world have all been shaped by these *pivot points*.

Pivot points are foundational events in your life when some kind of occurrence becomes a flash of insight that leads you down a path and lets you make a choice that significantly affects your life outcomes. Every exceptional individual can identify pivot points that shaped them, motivated them and got them started on the right track.

Even though pivot points occur during the formative phases, they play such a critical role in shaping the lives of exceptionals that, even decades later, they remember the impact these moments had on their lives. Pivot points instil a deep desire to accomplish something special and are motivating forces that drive you toward your goal. You'll hear those opportunities knocking on your door, and to become exceptional, you must choose to answer.

As events, experiences or actions that prompt you to take action in a certain way, pivot points can be positive or negative. Sometimes you may need to make a crucial choice or you may do unexpectedly well at something, exposing a skill you did not know you possessed. Many exceptionals can point to the first time they realized they were better than others at something, and this gave them a sense of gratification that motivated them to continue to get better.

One brilliant and renowned mathematician (who was anonymously quoted in a study) recalls that his pivot point was winning a ninth-grade math contest quite unexpectedly.[38] Not only was he surprised but even the instructor was taken by surprise and had him take another test just to be sure he really won. This is the pivot point

---

[38]Dr Benjamin Bloom, ed., *Developing Talent in Young People*, Ballantine Books, 1985.

that helped vault the young student into being one of the leading mathematical authorities in the world.

Pivot points are often external events that significantly shape your life choices. They may be opportunities that you can't let pass and believe you have to take advantage of. For Bill Gates, who was a student at Harvard University at the time, it was his friend Paul Allen showing him the cover of the January 1975 issue of *Popular Electronics* magazine that featured a new computer. This was the pivot point that marked the end of his college career and the beginning of Microsoft.[39]

Sometimes a pivot point simply occurs in your life as a random, everyday event that you may not ordinarily give a second thought to. Noted Seattle Symphony cellist Meeka Quan DiLorenzo recalls telling her instructor when she was 13 years old that she wanted to become a professional musician, even though at the time she had not exhibited any traits of being special or gifted in any way. The teacher simply replied, 'Sure, if you want to, but you are going to have to practice three hours a day if that is your goal.'

She took that up as a challenge, with her 13-year-old mind thinking that all she had to do was practice three hours a day and she could become a professional musician. At the time, no one believed she would actually practice for that long, but the next day she set up her clock and decided that she would practice for exactly three hours.

---

[39]Bill Gates, 'What I Loved About Paul Allen.' *GatesNotes*, 16 October 2018, https:// www.gatesnotes.com/About-Bill-Gates/Remembering-Paul-Allen. Accessed on 1 August 2020.

For someone used to practicing 20 minutes a day, filling up three hours was hard. She didn't even know what to do in a practice session for that long, so she developed a plan to fill those three hours that included a lot of repetitions and learning new skills. Soon enough, she realized she was getting better, and this motivated her to keep going and eventually become a world-renowned musician.

Pivot points may occur at any time and they may appear as serendipitous events such as when you start a new job, get a new coach or work with a new team. In reality, these occurrences are simply exposing your latent desires of things you want to accomplish.

Sometimes pivot points are negative life events—a professional setback or a failure that serves as a wake-up call. But even though the experience is negative, the impact it has on you is positive as it drives you toward a state of higher achievement. Many exceptional athletes who are in a slump or recovering from an injury feel a spark or extra bit of motivation when the people around them have given up on them. We often hear about athletes with a chip on their shoulder, who have something to prove because they were overlooked or because someone wrote something negative about them, or wrote them off altogether. These negative experiences serve as the supreme motivator.

Being motivated to prove doubters wrong is not limited to athletics. Every profession has people who use negative experiences as pivot points to achieve positive outcomes. Sometimes a negative pivot point is something truly tragic or catastrophic, such as losing a parent or other loved one that creates a void that is filled by a drive for excellence.

Identifying Your Pivot Points

The exceptionals can identify the pivot points that shaped them, motivated them and gave them a sense of purpose and desire to become the best at something. We all have those moments that give us a jolt where we think we can achieve something spectacular. But what separates the exceptionals from everyone else is how they react to these moments.

When we experience pivot points, the elite among us make a commitment to themselves that leads to a deep desire to succeed, an unmatched drive for achievement and a plan for specific actions toward achieving the goal. The rest of us feel the desire and pang for success when we experience our pivot points but we often do little or nothing, and quite soon, like every other experience, these pivotal moments simply pass.

The good news is that pivot points are not a once-in-a-lifetime occurrence. They happen frequently. They serve as catalysts that prompt action for things you really want from yourself anyway. You have certain goals, aspirations and ambitions, and the pivot points simply highlight them and expose the desires you feel and want to pursue. This means that Bill Gates and Paul Allen would still have founded Microsoft and had the same degree of success if they had not seen the *Popular Electronics* magazine; there would very likely have been another trigger.

The road to becoming exceptional is long and arduous and is one that most people believe they can't navigate, leading to a strong desire to quit. Fortunately, pivot points remind us what we really want to achieve. When you feel that twinge of desire pulling you in a certain direction, you need to follow through on the urge. Most likely, it is a pivot point prompting you to do something special. So, grab a hold of that pivot point or opportunity when you hear it knock, but don't beat yourself up for missing it. If it is something you really want, one will appear again soon. The impulse to strive for something exceptional is not a one-time urge. If you really want something, the signs will be there throughout your journey.

If you can use every spark you experience to keep you going forward, the road to becoming exceptional will become just a little bit easier.

THE PROGRESSION OF EXCEPTIONALS

The work done by Benjamin Bloom and his team of researchers sheds valuable insight into how exceptional talent develops.[40] Bloom and his team studied the talent development process of the most successful people across a broad spectrum of domains that included elite mathematicians, neurologists, swimmers, tennis players, concert pianists and sculptors.

Every participant whose life and career progression

---

[40]Dr Benjamin Bloom, ed., *Developing Talent in Young People*, Ballantine Books, 1985.

they studied met the strict bar of being exceptional. Swimmers had to be Olympians, tennis players had to be top-ranked internationally, mathematicians were winners of the Sloan Prize in mathematics and concert pianists needed to be finalists in one or more of the major international competitions to qualify in this research. Neurologists had to be among the most widely cited researchers and the sculptors were equally talented, having won a Guggenheim Fellowship and a National Endowment for the Arts award. Every individual who participated in the project was clearly among the best of the best.

The research team interviewed these exceptional individuals along with their parents and significant teachers and coaches who shaped and nurtured their talent as they developed. What the researchers learned reflects much of what we have discussed so far in this book.

The exceptionals in the Bloom project grew up in settings where their learning was supported. Most athletes, artists and researchers grew up in environments where sport, music and intellectual activity, respectively, were encouraged. Many of them, especially the future pianists and tennis players, started at a young age, and their talents were on display early and they soon began to specialize.

In other instances, such as for mathematicians, it is impossible to specialize at an early age. No one commits to being a mathematician when they are 10 years old. These children, however, were raised in an environment where academic achievements and intellectual behaviour were emphasized and valued. The questions they asked were treated seriously and when their parents did not know the answers, the children were taught how to find them.

Regardless of domain, a common theme that cut across all of these extraordinary individuals was that the environment they grew up in fostered a strong work ethic. They mainly came from households where hard work and discipline were expected, and parents set the example by exhibiting these qualities themselves. These individuals grew up understanding and valuing the importance of success and achievement, and the value of doing the best you can at all times was instilled at an early age.

None of these exceptionals achieved their success independently. Teachers, coaches, parents and mentors were crucial to their learning at all times during their development. The initial teachers made learning fun and taught them elementary skills. As their skills progressed, they soon outgrew the capabilities of their early mentors and teachers and needed more specialized learning to grow.

As they outgrew their earlier instructors, peers and coaches, they found new ones to teach them advanced skills. The new instructors and mentors not only worked on functional skill development, but also encouraged these budding exceptionals to strive for a high level of achievement and to think big. As their skills progressed, these individuals became increasingly committed to their disciplines. They had a deep desire to excel and to see how far they could go. Their friends and the people they spent time with were in the same field, and they collaborated with and competed against them. By this point, they identified themselves with their area and considered themselves mathematicians, swimmers, tennis players or pianists.

They were devoting upward of 25 hours per week on practice and skill improvement, and as they got better, they started reaching the borders of becoming elite performers. At this point, while they maintained their deep desire and motivation to become the very best they possibly could, their focus on pure skill development evolved to a more holistic view of the bigger picture. Instead of concentrating solely on technique, they thought about strategy and performance. They wanted to learn from the most accomplished people in their fields, as well as from people in other fields. They surrounded themselves with people who had attained high levels of success, observed them, and continued learning from them.

The process from showing early promise to becoming one of the greats is a long road that often takes years, if not decades. Each exceptional journey is different, but they all share common elements and themes. You, too, have an enormous amount of potential, but if you are like most people, you will squander it away. Wouldn't you want to know what would happen if you were able to harness your potential and take control of it? How far could you go? What level of accomplishments are you capable of achieving?

A LONG AND WINDING ROAD

The road to becoming extraordinary is not linear; it is a jumbled, winding journey filled with dead ends, spurts and restarts. No two paths are ever the same and every individual trek has its twists and turns. Sometimes it's not even the things we do that lead to immense success; events outside of our control (such as luck) may contribute to exceptional outcomes. But as we have learnt, these instances are rare, and the broad elements of excellence and the sequence of progression are common across most of the exceptionals.

Your unique traits are essential and help determine how far you can go, but when you understand and apply the common factors that are present in every journey to the top, your chances of becoming exceptional increase substantially. While we are enamoured by the achievements of exceptional people we read about or see on TV, you will get the same rewards and feel the same sense of gratification when you reach the top of your profession. You don't have to become a household name to experience that incredible feeling of achievement. You feel it when you become exceptional, or in other words, when you achieve your possible best.

10

DREAM BIG

When you decide that you want to achieve something spectacular during your time on earth and are committed to realizing your aspirations, you will already have attained a level of clarity and purpose that most people will never experience. The clear picture you carry in your mind of the significant goals you are shooting for becomes a rallying cry for you and everyone around you.

Aiming for something so grand is like deciding to put a person on the moon. You achieve success not because it is easy, but because it is so difficult that few are even willing to dream that big. But when you believe that you can do something remarkable, then everyone around you begins to share the same belief, and soon, the improbable becomes probable. When you start to see the results of your efforts, you enter a positive spiral that lets you improve exponentially rather than incrementally. As that happens, the unachievable is soon within reach.

You can follow the principles laid out in this book to develop the strategy and actions that are specific to you, but in summary, here is a set of steps that can help you on your journey.

STEP 1

If you exhibit talent in an area or know that you are gifted at something and are clear about the domain within which you wish to excel, you are already halfway along your journey to becoming exceptional. You can build from that. But remember that all raw talent can do is give you a dream and the occasional taste of what it might feel like to be excellent at something. If the journey to the top is a road trip from the West Coast to the East Coast, talent alone will take you to somewhere in the Midwest. Yes, you will have made a lot of progress but you would still be stuck somewhere in the middle and it might feel like the final destination is just as distant.

If you don't know what your gifts are, find them. You have to believe that you possess a set of talents in which you are superior and naturally gifted. Maybe you have to dig deep and perhaps you need to do some thoughtful introspection and soul searching, or maybe you need to ask others around you, but you need to uncover *your* special abilities. Without them, you can become good but never great. You have specific capabilities or intelligences that are more refined than others. Your journey to becoming exceptional should begin with identifying and building on them.

STEP 2

Once you identify the domain in which you wish to become exceptional, you can begin your transformation. The first thing you need to do is to paint a picture in your mind of what you believe you can achieve. Define your *possible best*. What are your specific targets? Develop a mental image and make it as precise and comprehensive as possible.

Then write it down. In as much detail as you can. Include how far you want to go, what you believe is possible for you, why you want to achieve it, how it will make you feel and what you are willing to do and give up in return. This becomes your personal declaration. You have to be honest with yourself. Don't feel shy about writing whatever is on your mind. You are doing this only for yourself. No one else needs to see what you have written unless you want them to.

If it will help provide clarity, get some assistance to write your personal declaration. Discuss it with someone who will challenge you and help you think clearly through the goals and aspirations you want to realize and commit to attaining. But whoever helps you should understand that they are doing this for you and not for themselves. There should be no expectations that others set on you. You will achieve your possible best only if you are intrinsically motivated. Writing down someone else's desires and targets will get you off track from the start.

Once you write your statement, fold up that piece of paper and keep it in a safe place. You will need to refer to it, read it and think about it frequently—maybe every day, every week or whenever you need it. But it is this repeated reinforcement of your vision that keeps you thinking about what you truly want to achieve, and what you are willing to give up for it. It reminds you why you are putting in the effort and prompts you to put in even more. Your declaration is a direct connection to your future self. In five or 10 years, the only certainty is that you will be either half a decade or a full decade older. But what your life looks like then and what you will have accomplished are mostly determined by the actions you take today.

STEP 3

Once you have clarity about what you want to achieve and have a written contract for yourself, then there is no reason to be anything but fully committed to attaining your goals. You can only be fully dedicated when you remove every other distraction from your mind. Whatever you wrote on that piece of paper should become the predominant force in your life. Your written words should be the force that drives and motivates you every single day. There is nothing else; there is no plan B.

If you are like most people, you may have established goals and a plan for yourself or perhaps you even wrote them down, but you have drifted away from them for one reason or another. Things that appear more interesting will always come along and tempt you to deviate from your path. Resist that temptation. Reread your statement and don't get swayed. Commitment means that you don't quit when things get tough.

There may be times when you need to switch direction or you may decide to do so. But if you believe that you want to become exceptional at something else, don't just flit over to a new life goal. Start from step 1 again. Find another area where you have the aptitude, write down your declaration, and make an unwavering commitment. The introspection that this process provides lends a level of discipline and gravitas that makes you more deliberate in your life choices.

STEP 4

You won't achieve your dreams if you don't believe you can. Having faith in your abilities is an essential driver of success. Even if you have everything else—talent, desire, effort and commitment—just the simple act of self-doubt can make that all for naught. A lack of self-efficacy is responsible for many potential greats never emerging. If you don't believe that you belong on the biggest stage, you will not belong.

Every exceptional has an ingrained belief in their ability to prevail. It is this belief that keeps them going. You may doubt yourself or face obstacles that you think are insurmountable, but it is your belief in your inevitable success that keeps you advancing. We have discussed ways to improve self-efficacy, most notably by setting and exceeding targets that are slightly outside your current capabilities. As you keep doing that, your belief in yourself increases and your achievements keep adding up.

STEP 5

Check to see if you are in an environment that favours your development. Do you have ready access to everything you need for extraordinary success in your field? You will only realize your dreams if you are in a setting that is designed and optimized to help you get better and reach higher. Beyond the physical surroundings, such as the tools and equipment that are available to you, are you surrounded by an aura of high achievement? You need to be in an environment that encourages the very best from you. You simply can't afford to be in a setting that permits mediocrity; you need to be in a place where excellence is expected and promoted.

If not, you may need to move. Perhaps find a new job where you can surround yourself with high achievers, or hang out with a new set of friends who reinforce that excelling in something is all right. Maybe you move to an area where you have better access to facilities, training or immersion in your domain and the ability to match your skill set with people more skilled than you. Your physical and social settings matter; make sure you are in the right ones.

STEP 6

You will not do it alone. You may think that you can muscle your way to the top by yourself, but it is virtually impossible to do so without a community—mentors, coaches, friends, parents—that can help you improve. Every field is increasingly more complex and extreme success these days requires the knowledge of multiple fields. You need to open your mind to learning new things and apply them to your field. New wisdom gets built from existing insights, and the more you can access existing knowledge, the greater heights you will reach.

Become a voracious reader and consumer of information. You will be surprised by how seemingly unrelated concepts from different fields can apply to your discipline. Knowledge truly is power. It is the most powerful tool in your arsenal, so get as much of it as you can.

STEP 7

There are countless little things you need to learn and refine to become exceptional. Most people invariably focus on the few things they believe are most important. But the margin between good and great is in the tiny details. Using a baseball analogy to illustrate the point, the difference between a .250 hitter in baseball, or someone who is average, and a .300 hitter, a mark of excellence, is one hit per week. That's all. It is not much. But the batters who focus on every little detail are the ones who achieve excellence. The ones who don't are left watching.

Microexcellence is a trait shared by every exceptional. They have broken down their domain into small and precise components and have attempted to perfect every detail in isolation. Then they have rebuilt and synthesized all of these microactions until the whole is infinitely more significant than the sum of its parts. That is how the best in the world have done it, and that is how you can too.

STEP 8

There is no question that you will need to devote all of your time, attention and effort to become the best in the world. No matter what you wish to excel at, you will not get there without investing an incredible amount of energy. You will need to spend more time, practice much harder, do a lot more work and show far more dedication than you ever dreamed of. Becoming exceptional is Darwinian in this regard, and those who are unwilling or unable to put in the effort are the first to get weeded out.

There is no secret here. You have to be willing to outwork everyone around you and certainly everyone eyeing the same goal as you. The volume of effort you need to put in is indispensable and there is nothing you can substitute for it. But, as we've discussed in this book, there are ways you can make yourself work harder—and with greater dedication and commitment.

AND IN THE END

Becoming exceptional is not just reserved for other people. Now that you have the blueprint that has worked for every person who has achieved extraordinary results, you can apply what you have learnt to your life. You, too, can become one of the all-time greats. All you have to do is get started and stay the course. The rewards are out there. You just have to go get them.

IN CLOSING

I hope you have enjoyed reading this book as much as I have enjoyed the process of researching and writing it. And I sincerely hope it helps you in your journey toward becoming exceptional. Working on *The Exceptionals* has been eye-opening for me.

It has shown me what I could have and should have done differently when I was growing up and in the early stages of my professional career. It has also given me valuable parenting lessons that I hope can assist you if you want to help your children become exceptional. We all want the most from ourselves and have the highest hopes and dreams for our children. With this book, now there are specific steps you can take and principles you can apply to maximize your potential, as well as help others maximize theirs.

I am always interested in hearing from my readers. If you have any questions or comments, or if you want to apply the lessons in this book to your life, email me at kumar@kumarmehta.com or follow my work on LinkedIn, where I will continue to post articles about how you can achieve your possible best.

You can become exceptional, but you have to really want it and you need to know how to do it. You don't have to give up on your dreams and aspirations. With this book, you know how the best in the world have done it—and how you can too.

INDEX